Praise for David M
Roadworthy

* * *

"True to the title, *Roadworthy* offers readers the world through the windshield of an 18-wheeler. But this collection is far more than a compendium of tales from the truckstop. The verbal maelstrom pulling the reader along through the poet's asphalt odyssey is psychological, mythological, and, at its best, disturbingly spiritual. His images are rich and keen not only because he has a poet's eye, but because he has a journeyman's wisdom concerning what to look for. The diction is at once figurative and precise, the syntax dense, the resonances dependably sure. Mehler has learned to pay soulful attention—and he demands that readers do the same."

— William Jolliff, Professor of English, Faculty Fellow, George Fox University

"These poems drive your mind through blue-collar ventures unaccustomed to literary affection—the world of long-haul trucks bringing shrink-wrapped loads of mystery along difficult roads to deliver the true texture of working experience. Here are revelations from the road, from long night runs, from alley dramas behind the Dollar Store. The poet reports on smoke breaks, road kills, Van Gogh as a working temp, the quick architecture of stacked pallets, bad jokes, poverty, commerce, trusty friends, jailings, firings, early snow and endless maintenance—all in a dense poetic line, 'a driven necessity badgering the mind.' You will emerge from this book deeper in experience, and eager to speak the poetry of working life: 'the trannies then were geared so low you could pull the pass in first and never spin a wheel.' "

— Kim Stafford, author of *Wild Honey, Tough Salt*

"David Mehler has produced a collection of poems illuminating a world that most people see only in passing. His rich, multi-layered pieces reveal the world of those whose lives are lived on our road, highways, and truck stops. Mehler's poems deserve to be read and reread."

— Geronimo Tagatac, author of *The Weight of the Sun, and Other Stories*

"In *Roadworthy*, David Mehler takes the reader like precious cargo cross country from loading dock to loading dock. He reminds me that truck drivers are my brothers—the human element in the supply train keeps the nation running for the long haul."

— David Memmott, author of *The Larger Earth* and *Lost Transmissions*

"For any of us who have spent long stretches of time working at a tedious or repetitive job, it can be tempting to adopt the opening line from Berryman's "Dreamsong 14" as an attitude, a way of being in one's world: "Life, friends, is boring." We plod along, head down, eyes blinkered, mind numbed. Mehler doesn't settle for this, heeding instead the advice of the wizened, crafty, old, truck driving sage in Ode to G.D. Winter: "'Remember, son—be attentive."' And, attentive he is, taking the reader, Sam Spade-like, through a twilit world that many of us, whether we shop at the Dollar Tree or Whole Foods, know little about and think of rarely. Whether it's a haunted semi trailer, a Van Gogh doppelganger, the vagaries of road conditions and other drivers, or the constant specter of mechanical failure, there's always an ambient sense of threat or dismay present, and no detail escapes the poet's eye."

— Keith Hansen, H&H Drywall

"*Roadworthy* represents an utterly unique lyric register built on an unerring sense of rhythm, speed and sound. In these psalms of the road, Mehler hits raw and wild chords, unlocking a hurting music we didn't know we needed so badly to hear."

— Gina Ochsner, author of *The Hidden Letters of Velta B.* and
The Russian Dreambook of Color and Flight

"In this book the sublime stays up all night drinking truck stop coffee, hoping to make it to the state line before sunrise. On each page, language and experience dance their inextricable dance, much to our pleasure and wisdom. Dollar Tree forever."

— Charles Hood, winner of the Felix Pollak Poetry, the Kenneth Patchen Prize,
and the Hollis Summers Poetry Prize

"In *Roadworthy*, David Mehler lets his many years as a truck driver roll fiercely across the page. In poems that double-clutch between a tender lyricism and a fire-hosed physicality, he brings you into the cab, over the pass, and right up to the loading dock. Mehler knows this work-grimed world and its many strange characters—and lets them sing in their own tongue, rough and sweet."

— Paul J. Willis, author of *Deer at Twilight: Poems from the North Cascades*

"Dave is a good writer, a good poet. By this I mean that he is technically good. His material reads as well as any great Hemingway prose. Hemingway's best prose reads like very good poetry. Dave's poetry is drier, more arid, somehow closer to what life is really about. Hemingway is great, but he can be pretentious. He is a grand man, and often speaks as a grand writer. Dave, however, chooses the real life of a long-haul truck driver and chooses to write about the characters who were not at the gates of hell. His characters are neither Captains of Industry nor war heroes. Or as T.S. Eliot would say in 'Gerontion':

> *I was neither at the hot gates*
> *Nor fought in the warm rain*

No grand cannonade in the neighboring forest of oak. Instead it is stories of people struggling with a real life of sequential cigarette breaks between stretches with a hand truck, a forklift or lifting with their arms and backs."

— Zeke Sanchez

Roadworthy

Poems

Dave Mehler

Aubade Publishing
Ashburn, VA

For Sally

Contents

III. Catalog of Joy

IV. The Hauling Witness

I. The Dollar Tree Poems

If I have a problem, it is this: there is a store where everything is a dollar.

–Gary Lutz

I bleed orange.

–Anthony, a Schneider driver on the Dollar Tree account

And he called him and said to him, 'What is this that I hear about you? Turn in the account of your management, for you can no longer be manager.' And the manager said to himself, 'What shall I do, since my master is taking the management away from me? I am not strong enough to dig, and I am ashamed to beg.

Luke 16:2-3

No Pirate, No Cowboy But Very Blue Collar, at the Dollar Tree in Eastport Plaza, Portland, OR

What I remember I remember being sent out
we were sent out one by one into darkness
a group of us sent out without any map always at night
it was dark and we would go out singly
and it seemed as if to spell one another and follow a line
but somehow I knew we always took different routes
a great arc or an orbit into vast wildernesses
was it forest meadows mountains or parks?

I don't remember any civilization
I don't remember any sounds streetlights bells or chime
not even gunshots I crossed a stream in my boots
and wore a greatcoat and carried a stick — we all had these
like a uniform the stick a staff of protection a talisman?

I knew or had been instructed that should I stray from the line
of orbit — a line that couldn't be seen by me
or anyone but felt or knew the route — that I would be
vulnerable because what I was doing was perilous
fraught with danger from creatures or forces in the dark
present but unseen and whether we were at war
or this just a fact of living the mission something
or someone depended on the simple task but don't remember
who or what was I struck by something in the dark?

And I never met anyone and I couldn't remember why. Later,
pieces of it float back to me in my coffin bunk and
again later as piece by piece rolls off
the truck to a crew stacking it
somewhere unseen.

Tiny Apocalypse Behind the Dollar Tree in Lewiston, ID

Behind the mall my truck faces a sheer hundred-foot-high cliff

running parallel with the back lot of the mall a hundred-foot-high cliff.
Strange how all these big-box stores stairstep

up the steep valley grade cut by the conjoining of the Snake and Clearwater rivers.
Just because the city grew. Walls formed by backs of buildings and cliff

become a miniature valley I must walk through to get from restaurant
back to my truck. Something inexplicable not rational unnerves me. Neighborhood fine

uneasy as if dark is full of intent even while security lights glow vague around
delivery-dock doors, overcast sky mottled grey black a shrouded half-moon shines through.

Hear some huffing noise a breathy intake then exhalation huh huh huh huh huh — too busy
relieving myself on the drive tires of the dark side of my semi to turn around

conscious rejection denial of alarm signifies courage or cowardice? First, owl?
Then something mechanized. Someone charging my back with a small axe this his war cry.

Still not turning — not willing to admit real threat not easily rattled but alert
hear the call again heh heh heh heh ehh. I see in my mind a throat feathered

pulsing rapidly with sound breath heralding something. Remember
working on a dock in Southern California hearing the sound of some animal

knife to neck screaming unearthly or infant brutalized in mortal terror — I asked Guillermo,
"What the hell was that?" "*Un Tecolote.*" "*Que?*" "*Pajaro grande,*" and he made expanding

motions with his hands and fingers circular around his eyes trying to make them look bigger.
"Ah."

Turning, I see the ghosty grey bird fly with wings white mottled on the undersides mirror
the photograph negative sky along cyclone fencing that girds cliff land to rest

on a post high up but directly in front of my truck. It is a cardboard cutout away
and above the light surveying whatever phantom scene exists on the other side of that fence —

I can't tell, or see what is up and over in darkness.

In shadow beside my truck, watch the head turning, both of us peering, eyes like black marbles,
sense more than see hunting eyes scrutinize, it sees clearer over distance curious

curious unafraid both eyes both sets calculating, individual equations, purposes, paradigms, then the bird flies away into the dark toward what must be

vacant field, round-ended wings, soundless, to talon snatch whole swallow squirming bite small wriggle furry bodies head first tail last like huh huh huh huh huh, the black throat

last nonsight for mice eyes thinking no this can't be, the horror impossibility this predicament no way out but down, down further, further in

— or off to cough up more bones in furry grey balls of pelt over and over night after night. Behind the mall my truck faces a sheer hundred-foot-high cliff and mice stream over the edge,

run toward it.

The Young Pugilist at the Dollar Tree in Milwaukie, OR

His face has this swollen-hammered look
unbruised but lumpy, eyes puffy
not fully open.

Standing behind the trailer he and the other two smoke
waiting for me to finish setting up: stacking pallets incrementally
higher making platforms, each step closer to the load,
over which I hook the rollers and lay them like track
together in a line forming a ramp

then finally take down the loadlocks and a strap
that secure the load against falling in transit,
drop to drop.

In the pause before the freight begins to roll
he tells the others a story, "My friend
had to get this emergency C-section but
just before they opened her up she said,
'Hey, long as you're in there can you fix it
so this never happens again?' " The crew laughs
but this is only foreplay before the punchline.

"She has this tattoo of two pistols here" —
his hands outline a pointy heart, index fingers V pointing
just above his crotch, bent thumbs circle cocked triggers
— "she used to be a stripper — you know —
I was sure they'd make them snub-nosed.
Somehow they made the cut,
took extra care to keep the tats intact."

Huge Photograph of a Logging Crew Hung in Burger King, Near the Dollar Tree in White City, OR

What you see, everybody must, sees who looks, is old,
them captive looking at you most—but not all—of course the stare
or jaunty smile see pride see desire, focus in on what you want to see
and feast away, chow down, no one twisting their arm then no
though you meet their eyes here through lens through history even long after death
years years years of time till no more except there, breaking this moment
forever, on this day at work soon forgot wearing soft hats posed around the biggest
fucking tree, momentous enough to photograph, they pause from work, silent—

the still and momentary ceasing of conversation, breath withheld, waiting
for the flash and pop—everything caught under lightning in the dark
they knew they must have known we would catch them so, naked dead
but undaunted to be captured thus, blown up, near the entrance of Burger King
standing around a larch over eleven feet the diameter and easily you pick out
the crew boss see there looking serious as sand or spilling secondhands,
money and daylight burns hat on straight all business, still, giving his permission—
near the middle some legs dangling over the cut tree rings slicing into legs—
sawn a frozen clockface exposing growth for what it is, we see but they didn't,
and the men with worn workgloves stiff with sap outside and oils inside
held or casually laid aside uncalloused like second skin pulled on and taken off
old growth wispy green like a soft wet kiss cool, but wanted . . .

A jigsaw beetle tunnel under crenelated bark, a river-eaten bank aimless but purposeful
all hardness all taunt of sawdust the men their sound gone, call from the underworld
a flat husky grey granulated *work work work   work.   feast away*—
that dream that kiss maybe some kind of gluey furniture now

a cougar's death on a blizzard-shadowed road

cubs paw and press and growling purr
wrestle muzzle closer in for milk
in a dry musky den close

by bracken creek moss willows stalk through the canyon

riverside gully wet dewy blades rained below the trees tented branch
rock jagged or flat along the Umpqua the green smell of watered fir

madrone pine scrub oak
underbrush or meadow musked with hoofed prey
which lies tender by

grassy beds rich the large cat dreams swift and slow

paws twitch as legs stride or jerk with crawl
through a creep or death leap

grown now mated she littered
now her own vie and play and dream
her eyes speckle-pointed suns

aged by hunt and the fallen dragged down by power hooked

a trained grace of claw and clench easy bite then perfect rip
jaw calm with wise instinct strong in awful youth

shadow always ghost only
passing prints a leaving
like breath or a sniff over snow

deer moving down from high country move in and drift lower

careless of cars in autumn food scarcer after first snowfall
a sudden whiteout pelting brief after dusk when it happened

road coated white in the dark
crossing bounded a branch snap
of light. Almost never seen hearing

unheeded the cat is caught by a machine that sees her but won't stop;

gold eyes stare into fifteen-ton light mid-bound broken. Blood
colors darker the muzzle, the blonde around the eyes.

God, even as roadkill
the face holds majesty
commands love and caution still —

as the blizzarding lulls, she heavily tail-dragged to rest on the shoulder, snow dusting,
back against forest, paws clawless point to the striated road

skidded wheels wet on whitened dark

Mene Mene Tekel Upharsin

Traveling southbound on my way into Portland steering
the big pumpkin truck, a gigantic tortoise gaining
ground on the hare, the tailgate and door of the little pickup proclaimed:
Conejo Couriers: *Rabbit Couriers*.

                        A startling word drawn, not scrawled,
but with what appears childlike or feminine care and legibility
by a finger in the dust on the black-tinted window of the truck shell,
                    in small case letters: *eternity*.

Smoke Break

I'm Nobody! Who are you?
> — **Emily Dickinson,** from #288

The three of them exit the warehouse,
huddle, bundled next to the railing just in front
of the large roll-up door, pull out cigarettes and lighters,
vigorously tamp their packs finally cupping hands lighting up
at the top of a wide concrete forklift ramp.

Banked on either side by rows and rows of dock doors and bays
to their left are dropped sea containers mostly from Asia
barged, railed, finally trucked in by Russian owner operators,
and common carrier trailers that represent the domestic incoming freight.
To the right are Schneider trailers, open bays, old leased tri-axle, hi-cube trailers
carrying on the sides and rear door the words, *Costco Wholesale,*
decals partially removed, but still readable.

These wait or are in process of being noisily loaded
with freight that's been picked, palletized, sequenced and sorted by weight,
then shrink-wrapped by these men or other lumpers.
All of this is organized, ordered by computers
operating corporately, networked nationwide, from a global buying network,
separating new supply and inventory into regions, individual
store deliveries, and finally into stops on a given trailer.
The computer is a labor slashing tool, another co-worker and task manager
logging spreadsheets and creating printouts to be checked and initialed
by operators like these smokers, the feet and hands
which become the Dollar Tree organism.

At the base and around one edge of the concrete ramp is a yellow wire
cage that houses the empties and the full replacement propane tanks
for the fleet of forklifts that run day and night, inside.

A light snow covers the asphalt, slightly melted,
no longer dusty flakes, but wet, icy,
and the snow has turned to sleet,
but these boys are tough — farmboys
drawn by work and wage — not warehouseman — used to it,
and they need their break, their nicotine, waiting
waiting for it, the burning charge, that marvelous relief of acrid inhalation
or maybe merely the punctuation of an activity — do some call it rest?
To one or all of them it is thoughtless compulsion that drives
the fingering the lighting the draw and exhale,
another kind of work. A driven necessity that badgers.
They all wear ball caps and heavy coats, one has a hood over that, face hidden.

Their hands, which must be cold, move toward their mouths
after a pause, then fall to rest at their sides,
then another pause, and out of a smile or in the midst of words
their breath falls out white,
a sighed smoky mix of life with death,
and another tumbling gently or in a stream.
Identification hangs from their coats.

What they are saying, a joke — gossip perhaps — bitching about so and so —
containing misogyny or crude sexual reference, fond belittlement
of one or the other of these three
about the work, sports, television
or the binge last night and hangover this morning,
who's in jail now and whether he'll be in long enough to lose his job over it —
none of this matters . . . because they're on break.
A cigarette burns in 3–5 minutes, depending on urgency or how far down you smoke it.

But on the asphalt painted with lines
and numbers hidden now
except for where dual tires from tractor or trailer cut arcs
which curve and intersect lines
sketching back a black calligraphy through a white erasure
in this regulated ballet of movement
of light over dark and dark through light
— not intentional, careful or attentive, but regulated. Entirely incidental. Beautiful.
And on the side of each dock door which appears in a driver side mirror
is a light blinking green or red
meaning ready or not. Wait or go. Stop or proceed.
Or green when no trailer is present, no work is being done.

Sleet falls, a snow covers, whitens the black
either hides the unsightly or washes it away after melting.
You decide. They watch the hostler jockey trailers now
— very fast very efficient, new empties put in doors,
completed ones pulled out;
work never finished.
They punch in and they punch out
another day.

Then, break over, butts flicked over the railing or into a coffee can
by the door where one of them punches in a code and the door opens.

My argument, sitting in my cab watching, goes like this: nothing is commonplace;
everything a brittle agony of import everywhere.

Someone must be in charge.

They load; I deliver.
Customers buy, customers consume: mostly the poor, looking for bargains.
All of us nobodies?

The tedium the repetition this misty futility a mask for what's shrouded behind it?

Because, in this same universe as *Dollar Tree,* ancient galaxies have collided
— will collide —
whatever wonders they were or contained changed in some crowded gaudy instant
of unimaginable light and gravity
like the projected light of it beaming away to us here.

Yet, here we are, still here . . . ancient
glittering creatures, made of the same stuff
as stars. Chiaroscuro. Complexity looking simple — *avia pervia.*

And 9 billion light years from the direction of the Virgo constellation
a gamma-ray burster sterilized that quadrant of the universe, but we are here.

Van Gogh Was Throwing Freight at the Dollar Tree in Oregon City, OR

There he was, all five foot four of him, terribly gaunt of course—but wiry and stronger than he looked—perhaps it's how large he has become in our imaginations but I expected he'd be taller. Just as I was sure it was Van Gogh, because self-portraits don't lie (do they?), I was simultaneously positive it couldn't actually be him. Obviously, right? Perhaps someone equally crazy wearing a costume with natural physical similarities—hell, I could play along. He did have the close-cropped red hair and angular features, and the first thing he did was demonstrate he wasn't afraid to climb into the trailer and work side by side with me despite the fact that doing so went against Dollar Tree policy (injury and liability issues). I admit, at first I was disconcerted: Could it really be Van Gogh? A poseur? Did I want a genuine or a fake crazy person in the trailer with me? What about that ridiculous straw hat he wore, decorated with many brightly colored ribbons? Apparently he didn't worry much for his appearance, despite tauntings he must take daily from school children for it. Most alarming, the missing ear (wow, that's hard to fake), but then you noticed splatters of paint on his clothing, shoes, his hands and arms, rings and flecks under his fingernails which were bit to the quick.

"You paint?" I asked.

"Yah," he responded, "mostly houses—my day job."

The odd thing was, the paint on his body and clothes weren't colors conventionally used in house painting, but why push it? We alternated throwing the boxes onto the rollers, which when moving quickly made a sound like a loud swarm of bees.

"I make my handful of francs here, for a few hours a week."

"Francs?" I smiled, humoring him, "You mean dollars?"

"No, no, a common mistake." He smiled, not budging an inch. "I'm Dutch, but moved here most recently from France."

"Ah," I said. If we were in California, I wouldn't even be asking questions—context would speak volumes. Okay. Sometimes Dollar Tree stores got temp help from the local rescue mission—especially in Spokane, I noticed. This never bothered me—any help was help. Still, dammit, after all the self-portraits, how can you not know a Van Gogh, when one is standing and working and sweating right next to you, muscling through the heavier freight? I began to wonder if something were bothering me—a bad sausage and egg McMuffin for breakfast? Something slipped into the coffee? He could tell something was nagging at me, perhaps it was because he was throwing two or three cases for every one of mine, and I couldn't stop staring.

Finally he said, "I remind you of someone . . . believe me, I get this a lot."

All I could think to say, dumb as it was, was, "Damn, you're a hard worker, aren't you? Passionate too. But tell me really, who are you? Actor fallen on hard times?"

"Color and light," he said, "light and color, always, even throwing these trifles out the back end of a trailer — as if the heaven between moments were all that mattered. We, you and I, serve the mundane, the tedious till it sparkles, eh, my truck-driving friend?"

Time to play hardball with this little fruitcake whoever he was, I decided. "But you never worked a day in your life except for a time as a failed art dealer, and at your art and painting. Your brother supported you tirelessly."

"Ah, now we get to the heart of it, then." His sharp blue eyes pierced me in the half-light of the dim trailer. "Perhaps I am working to pay off my debts, which are many . . . many. Or perhaps I am not the man you take me for — seriously, after all, how could I be — but honestly, how could I be anyone else? Could you be mad? Are you merely stupid? Something else? I cannot see or believe for you. Perhaps I am, as I used to think of my life, on a voyage in a frail boat in perilous seas? Or perhaps I was like a man who poured so much life into my pictures I neglected to live, in fact somehow" — he laughs — "confused painting with life, until now. Every day is extraordinary and we pilgrims sorrowful yet always rejoicing." Despite my no-nonsense attitude, as I looked at him, he began to shimmer around the edges — not exactly lighting up, but brightening and blurring a bit around the edges, as he took the hat off and mopped at his brow. I thought about how little sleep I'd gotten last night. As we finished and he turned to walk to the edge and then jump nimbly down from the trailer, he pointed to the propaganda poster on the warehouse wall. "Make every dollar count." I said, "Hey, thanks for the help today." He waved and nodded, then turned a corner, without looking back, heading for a smoke or a drink of water, no doubt. I placed the loadlocks and tightened the strap, lowering the rollers to the floor and feeling very tired, but my head was strangely buoyant and light, like a fever was coming on.

Sehnsucht and the Beautiful Girl of the Mill Town at the Dollar Tree in Springfield, OR

for George Brew

Like stranger leaves many-eyed, golden glowing higher
branched oak breezy and greens waft a wave,
swerve of undersea plant purplish grace reeling

weeding willow a last watery yellower light like this,
beauty such an alien solo thing seen prime,
extraterrestrial, so she stands fair, blonder

her black clothing well-fit and sleeked such —
then shed jacket bares shoulders shorn
striped by straps from black bra and camisole.

We've become hot backroom casual, her arms cock
to lift hefty, heavier cases of laundry soap I throw her way,
stack detergent, the short yellow hair caught and tufted

banded tight in back, lips take breath a curvy
red at fast pitch, below paired pale looks, bluish and
grey flecked below darker strips; calm browed.

A twilight slides inside the dawn after a sun-soldering arc —
she moves bending then through a curtsy
to catch deft fingered (while the plainer girl speaks)

fallen freight, such mild trouble seems delight,
her sleeveless sheen through the doorway
after a bottlenecking, caught me pause

to watch and not turn away (the other girl unsubtle
rounder yet squarish, offers coffee) her smile guesses
this beauty to me so somehow noisy becomes a flap

of thirty flocked doves taken flight,
or fish school silvered rainbow
collaring this way, that,

or grey and white-edged pigeon tail
wedges rising, feathered arms, handless, yet still
fingered, stretching to sky as one animal

pretty in symmetry and parts kind
firm fixed youth a taunt, comprehension full
she gives herself away to us mere

generous in skin smile the warm sight of her
looks and eyes blueing different each time
but silent staying, saying only what work says

to do, finish, then do again, we eye-hooked,
haunterling, me all hobbly stupid some big
sea bass baited barb set through gill,

netted up from such great depth this hungry
ached from under aching and
life sweet but bitterly changed and changing.

Night of Three Dreams and Tropical Wind

There are few more depressing sights than white sails falling about in the green darkness of a tropical night.

—Miles Hordern

Before the Columbia turns west it comes down from the north, smaller,
and bisects the state in apple orchard country north of Wenatchee.
18 degrees the night before in Ephrata, roads are slicked white
but sanded, the air hazy with diffused cloud snow, the river a calm grey steel
and the hills and mountains on either side are white broken by black of trees.

On this road I travel from Omak to Wenatchee to unload my last drop, unable
to not confess its frightening beauty to any, or myself. By the time I've offloaded,
it's already warmer, less frigid than wet, but by the time I roll onto I-90 the clouds
in the west blacken with murderous intent north—somewhere it has got to fall. I fuel
in Ellensburg then head south—by then it's dark, even so a sunburned cloud hangs

deepening. Between here and Yakima are large hills to climb deep valleys
to descend but the snow reflecting moon lightens everything, sky clearing,
and the Pineapple Express roars through; a warm high wind buffets my empty trailer.
Even so, I'm cheered traveling south and warming after all that arctic bullshit; beauty
brightens everything. By the time I reach Toppenish, I'm doubting my thermometer.

Following US 97 I'd crossed the bridge spanning the wider Columbia on its way to the sea,
stopping to land in one of the empty lots down the side road few knew about. A small
distance away all the other trucks clogged the Pilot parking lot at Biggs Junction
on the Oregon side. The wind started in earnest around 1 a.m., never stopping.
50 degrees outside—as if January turned to June overnight.

I. Cash

Driving down a rutted grassy road, the car ahead of me stops, inhabitants
thinking they are unobserved, while someone gets out and places several stacks
of cash at various points along the rut, the number of bills varying in height
but thick. I follow behind picking them up. I know I've picked up some of them
and the amount of money astounds, but once I get where I'm going, I regret it,
because I know there must be more, either because I saw there were and hadn't then
wanted to be greedy, or I'm just guessing. I can't wait to be done
with whatever it is I'm supposed to be doing in order to go back to retrieve
the money I missed before anyone else comes along.
The question never occurs to me
to ask who these people are in the car,
or why they leave behind stacks of cash—
That is, until I wake up.

II. Two Sisters

Numinous or lucre, they draw my fingers to dig at the base
of the porch steps, find them buried under the sand — unearthed stones
varying in size, all polished, red or white veined, agaty, some too large
for a tumbler but polished anyway, fist sized. Some bluish-white
surface a glow like pearl or opal, pocked like meteorite; finding, digging
more and more. Someone, sibling or friend, I don't know who, appears
by my side to finger and share the find. Unwillingly, I forfeit a portion.

Then, I see two sisters standing in a boat pour the rocks from a bag
into the Walla Walla River. It must have once passed over this place,
migrating, as rivers do
covering the stones in sand
to be discovered later.

III. The Annoying Lady

Most memorable was this, the one that startled me awake, disturbed:
I am escorting a woman by night, the path treacherous with large chunks of ice.
She is not elderly but older than middle-aged, not infirm, slightly overweight and nice enough
but one who talks too much, and I am helping her more out of kindness than obligation.
Perhaps duty. Perhaps she is a customer, but I offer the service gladly without
complaining. At some point she gets washed under — ice suddenly melts, something
like a dam breaks, and she is knocked over by the tide of cold cold water, then
comes up sputtering, upset and letting me know about it. I pull her up and we move on,
all the while exclaiming loudly how cold it is, how I should not have let her go and
of the suddenness of it all. *Dear oh dear.* We climb over chunks of ice, boulder size;
it's dark, either dawn or dusk isn't apparent. I help her to higher ground, she leading
the way, while someone, a man, appears at her side above me helping her up. I look
over my left shoulder, to see what looks like an eruption at Kilauea — a wide overwhelming
flow of magma just below the surface of all the ice and headed our direction . . . odd, but no steam
mars visibility. I understand it must have been this which caused the sudden melting of ice
to water that caught the annoying lady under. I think to myself, "This is it." Still, I would like
to climb up and get to higher ground, but the annoying woman and the man obstruct my path
and won't move. We stare, dumbfounded. I think about running away from the flow
of onrushing lava but seem unwilling to abandon the woman. I don't know why
this would be wrong but stand still thinking, bemused, terrified, *this is it.*
It occurs to me that the thing to do when it arrives would be to dive headfirst, under,
as though I were a surfer, trying to get beyond the rough breakers to larger calmer waves
further out away from shore.

Epilogue

The restless night rocked the truck back and forth
and I felt as though I hadn't slept. I bought
coffee and a cherimoya at the truckstop,
then headed west along the Gorge into the yellowed
morning landscape toward Portland, buffeted.

Dollar Tree, Longview, WA

After the setup, backing, then climbing down out of the cab
I heard a cry, muffled by bone or time or concrete,
or what I hoped might be that of a distant seabird, something
you hear, then call back, wondering if it was actually heard at all, or
merely some stray thought bubbling up through the deep earth of the mind
of dreams and dark early morning too soon after sudden waking
forced by alarm and schedule to rise and work—I paused waiting—but all
of this quickly washed away by cheery smells of frying eggs and bacon.

Then I heard it again, damn, still unexpected, coming unlistened for,
trying for my attention but still no more convinced it was audible.
To my right is fence and open parking lot, to my left is the back
of a Rent-A-Center building—could she be manacled to the wall in there,
tortured by bent psychopaths teaming up in some false-walled back room,
my chance to turn hero, exchange sweat-stained grubby clothes for a cape
and bright two-toned colored tights. No, too unlikely. Yet, echoing in the ear
of my mind the sound was like a roar from a captive in the bowels of the earth

burning in flame on fire for a thousand years beyond desire beyond
despair bathing in ice that scorches dry but surrounds like blood drowning
but never killing forever. A cry a scream the roar like that, twice. What can I,
who is among the living, do for her? Once, here, I heard a bird cry out twice
in nearby branches, startled awake by tentative drops which turned into a clatter
of downpour on the steel roof of the trailer. Now I and the startled bird strangely
have become one; small, startled waking, seeking shelter? After the unload,
I step across the alley for coffee and breakfast.

The Dollar Tree, Tacoma, WA

Sometimes the sun shines on a spring morning
and sometimes the world is beautiful.
Cars whisper by or roar innocuous, unmuffled perhaps, but
without rage, hustle, or aggression out on the boulevard.

The cop idles his patrol car, exhaust pipe steaming little clouds, ready
for anything yet relaxed as he sips from a green liter bottle of water or Sprite—
standing by conferring with someone in a work van
parallel parked head to tail like horses in a meadow
informed of some late mellow news.

A military cargo plane flies low straight over my truck
a ship of airborne rumble and metal rattles what's below
on the ocean floor of dry asphalt; warmth and sunshine
while I smoke, drink black coffee in the cab taking it all in
waiting on the freight crew to show up and ready the back room.

The local station streams great jazz cuts through the air
a river of sound one seeks, then finds, tunes into, perfect timeless,
selected for a morning program after being improvised on some smoky
close night where each breath is a miracle in some collective and individual musical mind
to become standard—new love, well-being floating everywhere over air
through light, now—just as startling later but in an entirely different way—
no longer joke or play or discovery but old genius—like the rarity
and anticipation of sunshine in a terminally rainy, cloudy place.

A recycle truck shows up, forklifts bales of recycle cardboard onto his
drop deck, all calmly doing what they're meant to this morning light airy
and I find, listening *My love is a deep blue sea, My love don't stand
for cheatin', She don't go for no midnight creepin'—you give me fever—*
all seems right. God must be in His Heaven.

Graffiti Behind the Dollar Tree in Coos Bay, OR

Instead of an alley or parking lot, the back of this store
faces a broad street semis delivering mail park on. Opposite,
at the corner is a large Harley-Davidson dealership
and showroom. An eccentric-looking elderly couple
always takes their brisk morning walk this way.

The flimsy rollers, cheaper than most sets stores have to work with,
must arc stretching, accordioned between a phone pole and its guy-wire support
to fit through the delivery doors at the right angle
                                       to receive freight from the back of the trailer,
and an employee always has to stand at the end of the curve
to keep rolling boxes from falling off—she is morbidly obese and hates
bending over to pick up fallen freight, but also fights
to keep the freight pushed up the incline of the ramp and
through the doorway to her co-workers inside.

There is palpable tension in our uneasy partnership
                                       an unspoken game in our work—
me in a hurry and she struggling to keep up with both ends,
frequently holding up a small chubby hand to halt me in mid-throw—
neither of us desiring freight to fall—
me for fear of damage, her for fear of bending over.
Freight wishes to fall because of being too light or too heavy.
Wordless, she huffs and scowls a lot, not minding if I see it.

A few steps up from the doors,
someone deviously clever and
                         bored has defaced the wall
with a jelly doughnut: first, they separated out with a fist the cherry
or raspberry filling, then threw it on the wall to simulate blood-spatter,
and in the middle of this, wrote with a finger in chocolate frosting,
"Hi," as if with shit.
                   The artificial color repulses more
than real blood and defecation might.
I wonder about this.
                   First, is that true? Second, my fat friend?

Spring, and a Mysterious Sense of Well-being at the 11th Street Dollar Tree in Eugene, OR

dedicated to Eli Holley

Standing foot-edge, trailer jacked west toward receiving door
rollers arc through it, like a fixed stream, water segmented, frozen, metal wheeled.

First drop—load bars and strap removed, shrink-wrap cut
on the left-hand pallet; setup complete; waiting . . .

Sun, heat and light tides amoebic, sprinting below darker horizon,
sensed as much as seen, a sky lightens, becomes kept memory.

In southern greater distance, dark foothills shift color, grey to green;
east, a car wash, where paired mallards stand mid car lane, just waking, preening.

Directly south and nearest, a slapped-together boxing ring covered
with corrugated fiberglass roofing used for kickboxing. Before the sun, the sky colors

gradual in non-drastic sky, even, slow attended so close you never mark changes—
like me like a machine doing precise work, water close to boiling—first the steam—

then finally beginning, we get started, but bored by this, still looking outward
wanting photography: drawn to the empty, silent square of ring, blank canvas,

padded ropes and corners, roof, on the sharp periphery: shoe brakes, open trannie casing,
parts of engines strewn, a metallic chaos, with bent fork tine wire edges

framing the ring's canvas garden. Behind the Dollar Tree dumpster,
a hovering canopy of recently greened-out tree overshadows the ring's fiberglass roof—

once done, I allow myself time to eat breakfast, and while inside, skim a paper's
headlines; glad of light, glad of yellow that bounces so warm off bright red, off yellow,

making plastics glow and clean, white tile waxed, floor bouncy, bouncing
people friendly, chats like the smell of hot, fresh coffee, then driving on to the next

drop on River Street remembering it was a rare, fine beginning to a smooth day.
Morning's horizontal light skimming with colors, and calm buoying, uncomplicated.

So it is hearts may beat and beneath the why of joy riding always underneath
this simmer of questions, inarticulate this sore joy seeping, underglimpsed—

Train, Bird, Man, Behind the Dollar Tree in Milton, WA

Despaired finally of describing the bald eagle's response, not as cry
shriek whistle nor even fluty laugh, no no no, but simply this:
the aspen splint of a Diamond Strike Anywhere kitchen match
scratched shearing into white bluish flame turning to mellow warm
reddish yellow—not orange—but red and yellow, burning just as sudden
just as long in a treetop over there somewhere in the dark, while the moon
hung its face just now behind a cloud, obscuring what light, till the eagle,
awoken as the laboring freight calls unearthly sweet rich loud awaaah
awaaaaah do you hear it awaaaaaaaaaaah he does waaaaaaaaaaahaaaaaah
echoes like some serpentine animal god wailing wound, metallic preeminence,
or perhaps merely, "I am here under this midnight sky, just like you." Unable to imagine
really, other than hear his reply, what such a bird makes of this (if wonder, curiosity,
annoyance) housed in his dark treetop standing in a less-than-acre fiefdom, compassed
by city and air—I hit on it, uniquely American, filled with like euphoria sudden
as sounds at night, or struck match. I scratch failure, I a part, like them,
articulate this dumb sound sounding, effort and afford, try to strike light.

Caught out of hours and regretfully handing off my rollers to Jim at the Dollar Tree in Beaverton, OR

"I don't like these Schneider directions—they're not clear."
He speaks through a grizzled beard,
weathered and burnt tobacco-ash wrinkled face.
Answers my question—me looking at the trailer, sizing him up
as he carries over each section of rollers from my tractor to lean up against trailer wall:
"Been with these guys only two months now
but at this for forty-four years. Used to pull a flatbed.
I don't like leaving my rollers out in the rack
exposed to the weather any more than I liked rolling up
dirty tarps—yeah I try to keep the rollers in the trailer.

"Still have two trucks, Peterbilts, parked at my house in Cusick.
You know I used to deliver to New York City all the time,
was one of the few who'd agree to go there. There would be three
exits with the same number, 6" — he smiles —
"and if you missed the right one or you took the wrong one
you'd either end up downtown or on your way to the docks.
If I got lost I stopped. I'd just stop, you bet,
right in the middle of a busy intersection, prop my feet up on the dash,
get out the thermos and pour myself a cup of coffee,
then wait for a cop to arrive. It never took long—hell,
they'd not only tell you how to get where you needed to go
but escort you out of there. I'll put a strap on these rollers
and leave them in the yard for you behind the guard shack."

He moves in closer. "I used to take loads to New York
until I got cut up. On the GW, he sliced through my air lines" —
tries to show me in the faint glow of a 4 a.m. parking lot
the scar across knuckles of a fist, then points down and motions upward —
"he stabbed me in the groin, here, like this.
They removed fourteen inches of my colon
—but I'll tell you what—I took that bloody knife from him."
Then he presses his bone-knobby fist just below my sternum, gently
presses in turning it slowly. "Only one of us went to the hospital."

Not the Chicken

I must prove I am not the chicken
not the chicken
okay

white feathers white feathers flutter bare
pink flesh exposed where feathers blown
off by wind and spotty thunder drizzle tire spray.

It fixed me with its peck of eye pecked
peering its eye through wire through glass windshield
the box tens of stacked rectangles cages rest

on a rolling rectangle platform a bed flat
rolling while behind feathers float a mangle
scud a skiff tumbling on the water wave wind

road dusting snowflakes midst a rainspray wind or
shed white wing feather unseen angels molted
only wake white breadcrumbs falling behind the flatbed

on a course to the slaughterhouse—it fixed me
but it's crazy that's crazy I can't be the chicken can I
and she can't be me still the bird

absurd somehow bargaining exchange—it for me that rapt
horror look said now I'm and will be the chicken
and her me I behind wire whip of movement transaction

both rolling between its misery and my evil station
misery for good but I can't be the chicken don't be
ridiculous but peck like at the inside of an egg says yes

it can no no no but the metaphor has already exacted
the exchange captive held bound wingless bounded
the chicken is now the man and man the chicken caged

once conceived trapped empathic held through wire
a chicken bone finger deepfryer vat bound
but first the plucking anyone anywhere anything else

I read roadsigns I remember my wife my kids I recite
from the prologue of the *Canterbury Tales* in Middle English
know nothing of dirtbaths egglaying I can't be the chicken

what magic what desperate wile
is this yet the metaphor ineluctable undeniable while I argue
this is not the natural order as we roll on in our metal cages

Sometime After 3 a.m. at the Dollar Tree in Vancouver, WA

I greatly prefer the company of the nuts, though
I will side with the sane any day.

— Franz Wright, from *The Lord's Prayer*

For some reason I find myself listening to late-night radio, on the way into work tonight—I don't usually do it because craziness has become mainstream—pervasive—why subject yourself to more of it for entertainment? But the twist is tonight's guest is a reputable investigative journalist, Stacy Horn, a contributor to NPR's *All Things Considered*. She has just finished a new book, *Unbelievable: Investigations into Ghosts, Poltergeists, Telepathy, and Other Unseen Phenomena* from the Duke Parapsychology Laboratory. She wished to write a ghost story, and this book would be a departure for her—also a departure for late-night radio—same material but a different kind of guest—someone sane and grounded on the interview block tonight. And she's writing and researching about studies and scientific inquiry done at Duke University. What? Turns out Duke didn't sponsor or officially sanction this but they did open up space on their campus for it.

There are plenty of holes in her story and my attention to it though—after all, I arrive at the Schneider terminal, leave my pickup, locate my tractor, rehook to my empty, then drive to the Ridgefield Dollar Tree yard where I impatiently deal with the inanities and ineptitudes of a security guard from the 19th century in age and habits who can't see or hear and must painstakingly peck at the keyboard with one finger after writing everything down three times in three different places, slowly. Then there are the commercial breaks which are always airing while I'm listening in the cab, but (apparently) much of the body of the interview takes place while I'm in the guard shack or cranking the landing gear as I swap trailers. What I catch is stuff about a naked medium, naked so one could see the ectoplasm when it came out from between her legs, Jackie Gleason's interest in the paranormal and desire to do a serious film project on it but could get no backing for it, Richard Nixon's correspondence indicating the government had alien remains in jars somewhere, most of this gleaned from the boxes of correspondence between the head and founder of the paranormal research lab, Dr. J.B. Rhine.

We learn that a poltergeist in a mansion on Long Island was investigated by a cop on the case who, while he was initially skeptical and annoyed by it, filled out exhaustive police reports that were hilarious in their detailed descriptions of the directions and measurements of the movement of objects. Rhine's theory was that poltergeists weren't noisy spirits but a localized phenomenon of telekinesis manifested from someone within a few miles' radius. Poltergeist activity wasn't something of emphasis because he couldn't reproduce the activity in a lab at Duke.

She spoke of the ghost in Harlem—a ghost story she chose to research because she had heard of it as a child—ten children get to a Revolutionary War museum early before the curator arrives and are playing in front of the estate, when a woman comes out on a balcony to tell them to shut up, then turns and walks back into the house. The children don't even consider it is a ghost, but truly believe it was a real woman—she is a little oddly dressed, but not translucent. Only after the curator shows up do they discover the museum was locked and empty, the doors to the balcony chained shut. Stacy Horn goes on to relay that she got this firsthand, after finding and interviewing one of the ten as an adult.

Most of her talk is on the experimental research done in a scientific vein at the lab at Duke. But then she speaks about desperate people, having tried every other avenue, turning to psychics to solve crimes, and is discussing the voluminous correspondence the lab receives. In one case, a boy goes missing, Bruce Crimmon or Grimmon. The parents are distraught and don't know what to do. They turn to the laboratory, who then refers them to three psychics, but they have limited resources. Two of the psychics offer information. One tells them what he saw, after conferring with Rhine—how do I tell these parents their child has been murdered? Some of the images he sees as a psychic are valid, other times figments—he is never sure until leads are followed and he is vindicated or proven false. He can't know or be in control of the information, except that sometimes it turns out to be correct. But he tells them. The other psychic tells the parents that the child was abducted by a childless couple who then relocated to Oregon. It's clear from the correspondence that this is the psychic they choose to put their hopes in, and while he is being paid to follow up on the case, there is no mention of what the amount was. Rhine, at the university, had urged the couple to stop paying this psychic.

Horn follows both leads and the name of the boy in her research, speaks with the mother who breaks down hysterically while talking about it even to this day. Finally Horn directs her research to the cold case file, but it is not there, which is a good sign—it means the case has been reopened. She is able to track down the detectives in charge of the case and offer them the letter written by the psychic who believed the boy was murdered. The detectives admit there is corroborating evidence in the letter but won't say what or how much specifically, and they go on to say they believe the killer was a man named MacRae, who eventually confessed to killing eighteen children over three decades and ended up killing himself in prison—they believe they know the names of three of the eighteen, but are still investigating the identities of the rest, which is why the case is still open.

As I listened to all this in cold, numb detachment—it bounced off me as just one more brutal murder—something we hear about almost everyday—the main question and focus in this lengthy digression in the interview was whether this paranormal stuff could be legitimate and scientifically or journalistically credible? She thought it was. The sensational is the theme every night on these talk shows but this guest seems not only to have a heart, but a mind, and even seems in command of all her faculties—this is novel—a new kind of sensationalism?

Next up the guests call in. But the show was riddled with gaps brought on by me having to do this and having to do that out of earshot. Now, I must begin unloading my first drop in Portland, and that goes smoothly enough—the freight manager is actually in the trailer helping offload the freight, while we listen to classic rock and argue interpretations of bawdy lyrics, marvel that some of the younger staff hasn't even heard of some of these bands—shit, we must be getting old. It isn't until I get to Vancouver—now it's a little after

3 a.m., and I'm deep inside the trailer, close to the nose, where the light isn't so bright—not dark exactly, but certainly dim—as I'm throwing freight, I begin to think about the story of the young boy—the reality of the abduction.

Maybe the catalyst is a yellow case of Dum Dum suckers with a marching band drummer and kids following depicted on the side. Or during the news in the break, earlier, that I learned of a two-year-old who escaped his parent's grasp to run out in the street where a hit-and-run pickup truck—thank God it wasn't a big truck (yes this matters) killed the boy—I shouted *Aw fuck!* when I heard that. Turns out it was a guy high on weed and cocaine. I think now this must have softened me up—overcome by the onset of a heavy liquid fatigue that isn't sleepiness so much as a deeper more bodily hunger for sleep felt in the weight of the limbs and at the base of the throat and bottom of the brain pan after forced and extended deprivation, just before hallucinations start up.

My mind is wandering. Suddenly what I see is a little boy, between six and eight—age if mentioned was in one of those gaps where I was out of the cab—and he is crying and saying over and over, *I want my mommy—please mister please—*and *won't you take me back to my mommy. Why. Why won't you. Mommy mommy, I want my mommy.* And then as if out of control of my vision myself I see a few different ways he might have killed the boy with a knife or straight razor in a walled off poorly lit soundproof room under the house, knowing he raped him, whether it was slow or fast, he saw it coming or not probably didn't matter—what mattered was the betrayal of being, existence, goodness and all he trusted in suddenly come against him—and in the depths of the dim tunnel of my trailer, I want to howl curses at the malevolence—weep, tear my hair cry a lament for this lost stolen innocent the parent could not deliver, and on whom God chose to withhold His mercy on a dank bronze LA night for whatever perfectly inexplicable reasons.

In my mind's eye I step inside the boy, I step inside the killer, then I step inside the boy again—take it all in, weigh both sides—

In the dark trailer, I could have been the killer, or I could be the boy. What if things had been done to me in such a way or over such a period of time I made all the wrong choices by becoming the evil done to me? Or, not worse but not much better, I could be the lamb. I could be a parent who backed over his two-year-old. Or tomorrow one who runs over a minivan with a family inside merely because I looked down for two seconds. I could crawl into the cab to sleep, then wake up in the nightmare of any of these stories, a future once in, unable to ever leave?

Last box out, finally, I step outside the trailer shaky like one after a near miss, unable to settle the fear. For a brief moment standing under the glare of the flourescent dock light, smoking a cigarette, I try once more to expel this mania from of my head. There must be some way out of this wilderness.

I must get back in my truck and drive before I sleep—but sleep means dreaming . . . submerging—giving myself over to strange, new, unknown realities. . . trying to find a way home, clean and whole.

At the Dollar Tree in Northbend, OR

after Bukowski

Woken by a cartoon horn
electric instead of air
but still annoyingly
loud enough
just in this sissy high register
checked my cell phone clock
3:13 in the fucking a.m.
I lay there
refusing to budge the curtain
a pause
then
BLARE BLARE BLARE
again
like roadrunner impotently
megaphone meep meep meeping

motherfucker wants to make a statement
well okay

finally get up
spread the curtains
see a Safeway truck
backing away into the fog
shit don't have my glasses on
can't read a number
on the tractor or trailer
no matter
time and company is all I need
his ass is mine

see him go around
through the parking lot
sure he has to dodge a car or two
Safeway graveyard employees
night stockers restocking shelves
bakers baking doughnuts
whatever

but to pull up to a cab
right up next to it
(for maximum effect)
blow your horn at three in the morning
know nothing about this driver
his day
his night

all you know
is that he did some little thing
to fuck with your routine
did something to piss you off

YOU

in your tiny
little world

tells me volumes
volumes
about this little day cab pissant
if he'd been a real man
he'd have banged on my door
until I got up shirtless
wearing only my boxers
if he'd looked me in the eyes
told me what he thought
but No
no
all he wanted to do
was wake me up
then drive away
the little prick
ha ha ha
not totally stupid

though
inexperienced
tomorrow I'll teach a lesson I
learned a long
long time ago
in my own little burned out world

you never fuck with another driver

it's to be avoided
especially in the middle of the night
when they're tucked away
in their sleeper
trying to get a couple hours of sleep
before getting up
starting all over again
unloading trailers entirely by hand
doing fucking mule and burro work
this is not the guy

you want to mess with
even if
or when
they park in your parking lot
backed up to the door of their delivery
the night before
when technically
they aren't supposed to
but wait until morning to back in
when the parking lot is already full
with parked cars and rude traffic

and setting up is much much harder

      * * *

hi can I speak to your store manager
you'll page him
good thanks
who delivered here
then left
at 3:13 a.m. last night
yeah
the dairy guy
okay thanks

ring ring ring

hi I want to register a complaint
with the driver supervisor of the region
would that be you
Yes sir one of your drivers
the dairy driver
who delivered to the Northbend Safeway
then left at 3:13 in the morning last night
he's got issues
there's an attitude problem
I've seen it before
pulled up to my cab
in the parking lot
honked three times
waited then
honked three more times
not only is it rude to the neighborhood
but dangerous you know
infringing on my hours of service
to interrupt my sleep

true I was blocking a throughway
I backed up to the door of my delivery
the night before
didn't know this was against policy
but now I do

yes sir he could easily get around
eventually he did pull around

point is and the bottom line
if he gets that angry over such a petty thing
treats fellow drivers that way
what is he doing around four-wheelers
other motorists
who may piss him off even more

I'm sorry sir but he needs an attitude check
I've seen this before
blowing things out of proportion like this
it means one of two things
dissatisfaction with the job
or burnout
he's a risk
a liability
for his sake
the sake of your company
and the sake of the motoring public
he needs you to review the situation with him sir
yes
I don't have to tell you that
for every incident provoking a call-in complaint like mine
there must have been
a minimum of ten others who didn't call it in
yes thank you too sir for following up on this matter with the driver
after he gets back in

you know
I wish I used a pallet jack to unload my truck
and drove a day cab got paid union wages

you wouldn't happen to be hiring
would you

Unloading at the Dollar Tree in Ellensburg, WA

This store is unusually located, downtown,
amid stately old brick buildings; parallel parked,
my steers and hood block a crosswalk.
Early morning late fall, thirty-three degrees, clear,
and from quiet leaf-strewn streets I feel a safe,
hot apple-cidery nostalgia. Comforting that a tiny
eddy of a town, a middle-America joy would rather die
than suburb or strip mall
                         —yet somehow survives.

Unloading, but during a pause in the racket,
I catch her saying to someone in the building,
"I woke up at four this morning, turned on *Animal Planet*,
and watched giraffes fight with their necks—man,
you shoulda seen the way they swung those necks."

Sign Language at the Dollar Tree on 182nd and Powell

Backed up against the wall so no one can force the door, though I'd feel it
if they did, who'd want to get out and investigate that jiggling of lock being cut
the trailer door opening? Risk my life for Dollar Tree freight? Not me, brother.
It seems it always rains when I'm here and early so sober white lights haven't yet
come on the black pavement wet always wet window down, smoking, listening
to a bird sing, somewhere just over the wall, to who or to what—me?
Don't make me laugh. Stare in front of me at graffiti tagging by toys poorly and
half done, on cinder block someone painting over another's, all of it amateur—
nothing pretty, nothing interesting—just a claim staked then rebuked.
Counting the beats of the song, two, three, again and again thank you
sometimes four—thank you sweet bird sweet sweet bird—why do it—
sweet sweet—surely someone figured it out wrote about it? Must google.
But perhaps not—the simplest things remain mystery do they not? Don't they,
well, so late in life sadly the first time I remember really listening this intently
trying to discern intent and surely there must be more to it than merely spring
so late or territory and why live here a pity for the poor thing but thank God
for them anyway here in this place where one night I ran over unaware
crushing the head of a rat the size of a child so fat no wonder it couldn't dodge the tire.
Another time a break-in, cops asking, did I see anyone coming or going up the alley?
And across the lot the bar busy, traffic, but I don't hear that tonight, I just know—
all I hear, repetition, birdsong, no one paying attention to it but me, this too I know,
and keep hoping for more and it delivers, keeps delivering, twilight song lighter
after the sun gone down. The three black guys who take the freight, marked all up
by prison or gangsta tats and spider webs up arms, over shoulders, fun and funny
they respect my blind-backing skills, want their own CDL, but I miss so much—
speaking as they do the language play I scarcely understand, gesture and innuendo
I hear more, enjoying the sound of birds animated, foreign, all brightly colored—
but of course first comes lightning then the thunder sky alive with force
like God's and surprise, His aseity, or a hard slap from behind. Once I saw
a beautiful woman dressed up all in black, high-heeled, about to enter the bar
as I was pulling into this lot—damn near clipped a parked car making my turn—
blind to everything but her at that moment. Struck lightning like that. Woman in black.
Ghetto birdsong at dusk in a light rain. Sweet, like a lover, spooning something
delicious to her husband behind the wheel of a semi pulling out of the truckstop.
Who can know it, where it comes from, when or why—sometimes, it just comes—

selah.

The Sunny Riverbank at the Dollar Tree Distribution Center in Ridgefield, WA

Check tee errr near the bank reaches high to grapple the blue.
I exchanged one locked room for another under this sun. *Didn't I*

Thinking I was moving forward in time; cafe for cab.
— *I am probably looking at this all wrong.*

The bird is telling me.
Telling me.

Black-winged shoulders notched
blood red — below red leaks hot gold light; *check tee*

errr sung among cattails abutted against this concrete lament
exiled, chastised – surrounded – calling my long gone

far
away home — and underneath this song this prophecy like pillars is
smoke for a garden fire for a city somewhere behind that blue.

II. Light Late Dark Early

A spring day too loud for talk
when bones tire of their flesh
and want something better.

—Jim Harrison, from *Return*

Under cover

we trekked to the deep dark woods. Raised up a room and roof of canvas. Cloth walls staked down at the floor with pegs through metaled eyelets, then lowering each window flap. This, next to a heavy iron grate over a firepit and a wooden table rough but overlaid by unfolding a creased, red-and-white-checked tablecloth. Placing then a small metal stove and a kerosene lantern with two tiny white socks that glowed and glowered and hissed, when pumped then lit, attracting moths. All thanks to the forward thinking of John Muir, a man who saw a cathedral where others saw forests—in much the same way centuries before him, builders of cathedrals saw stone forests and moving light through leaves become storytelling windows. But here and then, we pretended automobiles finned like rockets ran on splitting atoms—our way of racing against the Russkies. Beds unrolled and laid across the floor were forest green on the outside and red soft flannel inside with images of roping riding cowboys and Indians holding bows and arrows. In those days, rangers dressed up like Indians put on a show by pouring flaming embers dropping thousands of feet over the top of Glacier Point, so that in the pitch black evening fire looked like water falling and outshining the brightly visible stars over the Yosemite Valley. My space-age eyes watered with woodsmoke and the smell evoked such archetypal comfort. Over the campfire we roasted marshmallows on whittled sticks. We played board game rummy with fake poker chips listening to the hushed sounds of other campers all around us, after dinner dish clatter, pans clinking, metal zippers being zipped, unzipped, bobbing flashlights and footfalled whispers heading to a restroom late into the night. It was dangerous, an innocent, a reckless time for disneyed children out of doors. We who, schooled by Pinocchio, Bambi, and Dumbo knew that even should bombs fall, a hero might arise—and children did drills and could duck under desks. The world could never nor would not ever truly end.

Spring

The black-lettered school bus
hisses up the oily street, stops
in front of slick yellow children
holding tight their metal lunchboxes

on a wet sidewalk that mirrors sky—
though the sky is still grey, the sun
makes colors flare—laquery concrete
and green of new-leafed shrubs and trees

rain bright and on every child,
a yellow slicker shiny new;
brass-buttoned rubber pants,
hooded raincoat with brass

clasps that fold and lock, clean
and squeaky from lack of use,
collars indelibly markered black
with a name. The bus arrives at

Amber Drive Grammar School:
the lever pulled, the door
folding sighs open—
as dropped-off cargoes splash

out, the schoolyard glares
smelling of grass and clouds.
The classroom, louder with rain—
slid sounds of shouts and chairs

on linoleum tile—the teacher hushes,
while the dark quiet closet waits,
hooked with yellow
dripping on wet lunch pails.

North Fork Skykomish Under Mount Index

A coldheap of greenblur bluer than trees
$\qquad\qquad$ that border up the rockcrag
loud white molecular phrases
$\qquad\qquad$ living words shouted
$\quad$ thought fed and followed
flies frothblown sheets of glass subduct
$\qquad\qquad\qquad$ sliding in horizontal fall
a lapwing awash ouzeled $\qquad$ shoving backlash
like Coho fierce to breed then die
$\qquad\qquad$ fish flesh harder than water
but less able to persevere than water
$\qquad\qquad$ or idea
abackreach race and powdery push
$\qquad\qquad\qquad$ waterflecks light air
and power push of punch onrushed
$\qquad\qquad$ force eddied still in frozen spin but sliding
this fractured green quartz aerates liquid
$\qquad\qquad$ swallowed bubbles churn sustained in roar
like curtain liquor slop to foaming racket
$\qquad\qquad$ over submerged stone
racked in heaps yellowed blue melds flux
$\qquad\qquad\qquad$ lighter shades of stones
stacking fallen movement
$\qquad$ flow

Cottonwood leaf $\quad$ splotches of dead
$\qquad\qquad$ disconnected from tallest boughs
shade green to yellow
$\qquad\qquad$ drops stem over leafpoint
$\qquad\qquad\qquad$ shimmies to float
finally to sink
$\qquad$ then run
then walk the bottom
$\qquad$ a legless current settling brown
green sheets fold and flex
$\qquad$ riverbottom
they scrub rocks clean

flat-faced standing boulder a blank grey headstone
inscribed by black lichen's slow growth
$\qquad$ offers no narrative but water

many things look like one thing

above Index broken cloudchip cirrus heelscuffs curved dents hang in the blue spent
contrails spit across skidding thirty thousand feet up

Skykomish means inland people
                                mostly underground
mighty river   or tiny town near-dead

one thing can mean many things

money must flow in from somewhere now

Great Northern Railway ran through the middle
                                    skirts the bank
like a white shaggy mountain goat painted
                               BNSF now

Outwitting Your Angels

Angels are of two sorts; best not to provoke either.

— **Scott Cairns, from** *Disciplinary Treatises, #5 Angels*

Use every animal ferocity be fierce as fire lovely fire they are made of and as willful
use blood cunning fear shrewdly corporeal rightly and against them.
They will not expect it either hate or applaud you.
You require oxygen fuel sheltering sleep, and change in time—alien,
they do not—but twinned to you nonetheless.

Use that. Be the compact wolverine squat underestimated
harried by hunter pursued across tundra over rises
who turns and charges knock him off his high loud horse
stop the snowmobile's white wings over cloud froze high.
Even before he can pull rifle from sheath stare him down unscratched unbitten
till he will not no cannot shoot you even in war as you turn away undaunted
make him admire you ashamed of himself.

Be a virus relentless soulless machinelike repetitive
producing like kind impervious fruitful godlike and love strange
like that—no antibody will withstand no death touch you for long.

Certain light heat lightning hot white quick or black black black he may shapeshift
while you the muddy cornered pooch pathetic you a mutt pup pissing
down your leg throat up back down saying here take it always outnumbered
always outgunned before you were born unable unchosen without gift of speech
a vague dream a bark a whimper only canine teeth barely a conscious being
no power of thought really no imagination as it should be truly understood

and they understand,

yet know in the Presence even they must cover their faces with haughty wings
still they superhuman cry they *other* laugh hear music your ears must be deaf to
you dimly uncomprehending sniff the air circular back leg scratch at an itch

unreachable not merely skin deep. But think, remember, did He identify with
did He die for them? His plan His image He outwitted He becomes the wedge
between you *kyrie kyrie* to your angel *eleison* you must look weak

must but the secret is this weak is the weapon they in hoary anger mirror
horrible harbinge dark ancient awe, these guests unwished for, unanimal yes
the doorway you put off opening the facade hot cool
cool hot layered the dog dressed up like death but you couldn't know
didn't imagine death and everything you lost every buried bone will
one day come back to greet you.

Overhead

A crucible a crucifix and a cross to bear a crocodile a tiger any and
all manner of sharp-teethed men a porcupine gnawing at the joists
and subfloor you try to beat to death with a shovel whenever he
shows himself. Roof shingles the rain beats wind buffets leaky plumbing
hard choices you are ill-equipped to make but make anyway fickle clientele
crazy workers the state economy voracious all of them always demanding
song pleasantry while sucking suing overtime sweat bloodletting dreams

subsidy on faith futures give give give get half as much back
costs rising faster than you keep up with vendors siege while serving
eating up everything bugs climate spiritual and mechanical pestilence
every kind of failure known and unknown factors itself in but the jester
keeps juggling and digging because a business depends on it walking away
no option humble knows no downward bounds surprising even the humble
power water food costs like bricks without straw and debt there is plenty

of straw indeed no last straw so many they will follow you into death
as you hurry to get past them just to work for someone other than yourself again
and get out from under by getting under memory and failure dog but overhead
like friendly counsel holding you to itself knows every weakness finds
which strength is faultily inadequate, meanwhile above, a recording angel
scribbles notes to himself ticks off each light momentary wrong of this little
spider picked off its web by a beaked and beautiful multicolor feathered bird

Moonlights

for Steve Parker

A nightmusic sky primitive a deep blue to black greenish nocturne
gold-dotted for lights no stars not constellations but urban sparks
firework across drop red spits here yellow there, over a wide river this
was and over a hundred years back painted by a whistling American
that dandy mustachioed yank outrageous impression like music
working without light bangsmudged and blotting dark soundless
pops punctuated by barest light and splatter dripping two vein red
lines emberglossed fallen over ship a sloop liquid garden brass
watermusic perhaps sootsmell maybe moonlight lit the wooden canvas.

Libeled he bet a lawsuit won a farthing but that damn Ruskin cost
him his fortune like a flaming shipafire: what is this ocean between
critic and artist? Beauty to us now but so much public other then
between comprehending taste likes in flux battles lit quench
riverwet retardant pulls against flame trudging fired shots dark
rage sprinkle out over black heavy inches caloried paint crackles
skyed words sound a skywardling night so brieflylit but fixed in time.

The Neighborhood at 2:22 p.m.

At the park a child wearing a colorful shirt spins and spins
drugging himself until sitting wobbly about to fall

while the man on the bench watches
poisoning blood and heart unthinkingly
with smoke daydreaming of sex

while someone up the road and around the corner turns a key
cranks a starter whirring but the car won't start
doesn't stop whirring just whirrs
cranking not catching the fuel won't ignite

and the blonde lady with tints of middle age frosting her hair
stands barefooted in a short pink robe shows off her legs unthinkingly
across the street talking to the foreman painting her house
and one shouts to the other time to break for lunch
one pays as another earns and this from top to bottom this is the way

as the suns shines a lighter warmth cuts past maple
leaves eating light for storage and cool breezing
house across the street sprayed a pleasant green coating
trimmed crème from patches remaining grey and under

while upstairs the mournful dog refuses to budge from the daughter's bed
he shouldn't be on and downstairs children play video games
as someone in the kitchen fingers the bottle
then pops their blood pressure medicine fretting they took it already

one street over the macaw's words are not
heard through glass but bounce
lonely for canopy and sound
his colors mean nothing so he plucks out breast feathers unthinkingly

all this work wanes
on a latening Saturday.

Monument

Black dark wells in rock
point to what once were trees;
immolated standing or fallen,

ancient ponderosa pines left lava
casts. Molten magma sidled
up to blanket deep against trunks

unable to flee the dancing heat and flame.
Unable, they became something other —
not martyr or stake they became both —

the swallowing pursuer makes mimick
what once nourished, then betrayed.
Leaving the trace of their futile stand —

pits — a howling hole; seared gaping mouth;
ancient absence. The only sound
a crying wind washing

around twists of trunk and branch
of children crouching, wary but still,
which inched through centuries

back over the jagged, black land.

Mid-January Early Morning Smoke

Low bright dawn fog on lake burning
off white after white after white up;

shadowy firs mirror up up hazed line of

Coastal Range and final greyish cloud; a train
sudden soundless over tracks

with hidden freight unknown, great clouds billow

steaming by; a gull skitters water, landing or leaving;
visible, a stacked rank of forest on a truck trailer

passes, to become something other.

Next, one grey bearded, ruck sacked,
hounded by cawing crows in his wake—

barely seen seed drops from his hand; he

his harried ghost ambles on away caring
for the unloved and finally gone like smoky breath.

Autumn Dread Winter

– to jackie

A ghost,
          to look,
after years wandering wastes and wild
                                        return
                    to a place while lived   young (husband,
lover, father) – now have none,   but then youth
flesh on my side,
                    for her.
Now and old   wraith return
                                        to memories mourning
this desolation stone schoolhouse empty ancient
dry.

Somewhere north   at hilly base   the Steens   under rock
sagebrush, haunt of coyote   hare   lies buried   tiny   bones
never yet calcified,   a miscarried daughter. Perhaps she
I might meet   soon   if only it could cross the river threshold. Kick mice
bony   an owl cast from several   then upstare   lightless   through barred
skeletal

silvered elm bereft branches
                            unleaved   shadowed of mountains.
Windows   a set   in stone
                    dark paned no door visible.

Someone said never look on the moon alone
                                        believe it.
Offers nothing but memory and bitter
                                        ruined for sweet
afraid it dare not look up. old   beyond even wrinkles
                    grey mottle
past ash
          to a nothing
snow.

Quiet Night at the Alvord Desert Bath House

The flat expanse of alkali desert stretches out white miles
before the moon; beer in hand we soak next to riddled tin
corrugated as a box barrier against wind and blocking sight.

We sit in the open one where the water is hot
hot smells of sulfurous mineral must come from great
depths, causing and washing sweat from cowboy and tourist alike.

Deep silence created by distance, only the hum of blood
running, trickling water haunts, so we laugh and drink then

to coyotes' yip yip joy of ripped red life: in our guts we know we
all are tourists here. Mike shoots off his .22 aimed loose and high.

Evidently

As vehicles of cold the waves on this wintry day are rough,
frosted with breaking foam hundreds of yards out.
Down the beach to the south the white orb of the sun shines harsh
through gauze — a hazy wall of light cloud illuminating waves,
creating a wash of blinding silver over wet sand, electric foam rushing in
to reflect directly into the eyes forcing them to blink or turn away to hide
— light unbounded, blinding — but luring the eye to keep turning back
at sidelong beauty. The ocean has that heavy brine smell conjuring time,
depth, the primeval — decay wafts and remnant evidences on the shore edge
imply multitudes beyond, luxuriant life and saline excess that must exist unseen
under fathoms in such vicious symbiotic richness, color and number
almost beyond catalog or description. The waves roll soundless over the depths
but thunder and hiss in drawback as water tumbles over itself, returning to itself
in pullback to wash over rock and sand, speak.

        Or what? — all this might tell us something we need to know
about God — or signify absolutely nothing but movement of earth, air, water
— communicate absence of care or intent — kinetic energy — machinations
blackly indifferent or as grasping as a people peering across a void
of telescoped light years to speculate on or name the gaseous dust of burning
stars brimmed, cascading their own ancient dying or already extinguished light.
        Maybe scanning for a new earth, atmosphere, water, in hope
or fear of some other more advanced civilization, thereby telling us
something we might need to know about God —
        or fail completely to confirm or deny. . .

III. Catalog of Joy

What about your shit pants fear? What about that?

—Craig Goodworth

But I had some fears:
the salesman of eyes,
his case was full of fishy baubles,
against black velvet, jeweled gore,
the great cocked hoof of a Belgian mare,
a nest of milk snakes by the water trough,
electric fences,
my uncle's hounds,
the pump arm of an oil well,
the chop and whir of a combine in the sun.

—Jim Harrison, from *Sketch for a Job-Application Blank*

A man carving his way into things,
holding the wheel,
trying to find his way home.

—Michael Delp, from *Killings*

If life is a miracle,
then death is, too.

—Richard Jones, from *The Waiting Room*

. . . there's gold in them thar hills . . .

—Carla Conley Chervin

Q: What scares you the most?

for Craig Goodworth

A:

Being on a steep-sloped second story roof while prepping and painting a house dormer.
Falling and dying.
Falling but not dying.
Paralysis.

Giving the job my all but it never being good enough
due to lack of skill or ability. Having desire
but not the resources:
the feeling afterward.

My daughter coming out of her three-year marriage
deciding she's gay.
Imagining what comes next.

Two spiders, one big as a fat fist, the other
smaller riding it, but with crab claws:
all sets of eyes looking into mine, swinging
toward me like Tarzan and Jane.

Dementia:
first, the realization. Then,
having seen it in others,
discovering *exactly* how it works.
Firsthand.

This happening to your wife first.
Or,
at the same time.

Or blindness.

Actually, any wasting degenerative disease will do.

Paper cut fears can loom like catastrophe.

* * *

The look on the face of the tech after an hour-long MRI of my brain,
half with dye, half without. Gauging her expression, noting
she's being nice to you but seems irritable with everyone else.

Wondering if it means anything.

Thinking, amidst the clanging—fifty-something-year-old brain—how is it possible they'll find
anything good?
Remembering the faces of the people in the waiting room, mostly accompanied by spouses for comfort.
Kenny G on the headphones (you requested bebop or post-bop) meant to drown out the hammering
sound and the claustrophobia looking out through a periscope device to keep from losing it,
knowing you are in a lower budget machine too narrow for your shoulders, and this is nothing
like the ones you've seen on doctor shows. Cold-hearted insurance companies!

(Why didn't you just request heavy metal or hip-hop?)
Hearing the tech say the expected: your doctor will call with the results in the next 5–7 business days.
Not wanting to know, but needing to know:

the pendulum swing between these, over and over.
Weighing the difference. Waiting on the phone to ring with the findings.

Dreading the ring of the phone with the findings.
Knowing that knowing might help you survive what's coming.

Also knowing your life from today on will never be the life you had before.

Realizing that dying before your life insurance policy expiration could be really advantageous.

Considering the medical costs.

Considering leaving your wife and children early,
especially now when you're maybe slightly less of a dumbass,

maybe wise enough finally you might actually be of some use?

All sorts of seat-pucker fears related to driving a semi:

Killing someone. Their fault or mine—doesn't matter.

Falling asleep behind the wheel.
The car under my trailer I didn't expect.

Animals on the road: deer, elk, bears, livestock.
Animals on an icy road.

Fog: Highway 99 in California, or I-80
through the Midwest at night in the hammer lane.
Both perfectly fine examples . . .

Spinning out on Wolf Creek Pass, fully chained, but it making no difference:
the helplessness of that.
Trailer's empty, in a cursed cab-over, everyone passing, speculating
over the CB why you don't have enough traction.

Idiots throwing jack-o-lanterns off
an LA interstate overpass, timing it
to hit the windshields of traffic below
and hitting some.
Finding this hilarious.

Or, merely the wrong part of Philadelphia,
heaved beer bottles bouncing off my trailer.

Snowing
on top of ice laid over the two-lane to Lake City when
a ghost herd of elk burst out of a downhill stand of trees,
crossing the road at a run, both of us unable to stop;
tried to slow the pup, asses brushed as it passes,
wakes of powder blowing up in a cloud sides and behind — mirrors show
no bodies falling or sliding. The forest and snow deep.

Climbing Eisenhower without chains when an SUV passes, skis on the rack,
loses traction doing 360s directly in front of you.
Still, not wanting to slow because you might not get started again;
letting off slightly, till they clear the hood, then throttling
after they slam into the snowbank on the right.
The craziness of this dilemma.

The 300-pound juggernaut; a set of duals in a wheel-off incident,
separated from the truck hurtling up the opposing lane,
so casually and slow you can't believe it
bouncing over the jersey barriers of the median,
watching detached as it rolls toward you at something like 55 mph,
waiting, watching, estimating vectors
unable to maneuver and taking forever.

Middle of the night . . . no chains, gambling, not hanging a drag
because you climbed the western side just fine:
downhill jackknifing the empty trailer
(emergency vehicles and flashing lights at the base of the pass!)
needing to brake fast
but needing to not jackknife too.
Hear that panicked voice over the CB hailing you, warning — *ohh shit* —
foot stabbing releasing light and hard a fast tempo drum beat the brakes.

No way out of this one.

> * * *

Fog bank on I-25,
where the road dips,
during morning commute
between Denver and Fort Collins,
roads icy because of it,
40 car pileups,
northbound and southbound,
hidden inside.

Wyoming crosswinds on I-80 with an empty trailer
laid-over trucks along the shoulder
sleeping dogs.

A malevolent four-wheeler spies
opportunity for a lawsuit
sets a trap.
Let's say a poor white-trash mom.

Residential deliveries in Aspen.

One scrape too many and losing the job.
Or keeping it, but losing your coveted local job
and being put back on long-haul for an indefinite period.
But not before training the new guy who replaces you
— likeable, cautious, accomplishing half in a day what you did.

Pulling into a blind wide alley,
downtown Salt Lake, between buildings,
no way to turn around nearly impossible to back out.
Turning around anyway
scraping grooves into the bricks with the door hinges
from the swinging back-drag of the trailer's overhang
Get out fast!

Realizing too late your wrong turn,
you find yourself in the affluent foothills above Portland — you're lost
and use a spacious residential driveway to back your pup into to get turned around.
You catch sight of the owner watching
scribbling crazily on a pad.
You cannot afford even one more phone call.

That Indian reservation in Idaho,
stopping to hop out
ask a couple of guys standing around
if they know where to deliver the fireworks,
forgetting to set the park brake.
They point and laugh, watching as the truck begins to roll.
You turn and run.

The off-ramp to your delivery in South Central is under construction
and your directions to the warehouse made useless:
Now what?

Flipping off a four-wheeler but a few miles later he beats you to the scale,
has time to complain, and you're called in to answer for it,
no time to catch up the logbook.
Turns out he used to drive for Swift . . .

Low bridges all over old cities like Philadelphia, Chicago, even Spokane,
rails running through them. People honking
to move me forward into an underpass with clearance too low
no clue why I've stopped, traffic piling up behind
leaving me nowhere to go to get out of the way.
This, well before cell phones, I must wait for the cops to show.

Crossing railroad tracks the rail-crossing bar lowers, hits
bouncing off the trailer, loud alarm bell clanging, red light flashing, dreamlike
— train coming —
— traffic in front and behind —
being that stupid that reckless; what a four-wheeler move!

Desperately needing to go (terrible truckstop food) but no place to do it.

Miscalculating and running out of fuel: fueling a calculated game we play because it
gives away time and location, like a sub to a destroyer.
Break-down in the most terrible spot: in the desert, some unpopulated place with a
windchill of 40 below, an urban center along a congested freeway without shoulders or
inability to coast and crossover to one. Being that superstar.

Then at the landfill:

A disgruntled employee armed and shooting.
I'm well-liked, but this place drives people absolutely batty.

Unfired ammunition shooting out of the trailer walls;
exploding boats not drained of gasoline.

Forgetting to hook the trailer after tipping.

Pinning Tim between my backing trailer and the tipper backstop
because he's old, can't hear, has his back turned digging out trash.
I failed to see him before he was out of mirror view.
What it would be like to walk toward the back of the trailer to unlatch the door
then discover him —
a few feet more that one time. . .but God (some inner voice) saved us both.

* * *

Buying a business. All this entails. Face financial disaster, public humiliation, failure
in this business venture. How close
to losing everything in the small town you live in. Shame, repercussions,
played out . . .

And here are a couple good ones:
Heart attack on a plane.
Shark attack snorkeling in Kauai.

* * *

Eternity.

Seeing the face of God: beatific.

Not beatific. Darkness.
Never seeing the face of God.

Facing the knowledge that not only am I being punished for what I did and didn't do,
and deserving it, but also that there is no way to set things right, no way out,
forever (whatever that could possibly mean).

Attaining the ability to truly identify with Satan.
Understand true despair for the first time to be truly hopeless.

Fears my kids and others I know and love may be damned.
Knowing I might have done something but didn't.
Could have intervened when there was time, but didn't:
of the variety of reasons, worst being cowardice, next worst laziness,
acedia. Of course
I didn't pray or intercede for them. Or not enough. Never enough.

Just generally being stupid, ignorant, thoughtless and left to myself to remain that way.

Forever.

      * * *

Giving a poetry reading.

IV. The Hauling Witness

All through my twenties I had two terrors: that I was going to have to get some sort of regular job, and that I would never write great poetry . . . I think of telemarketing in Seattle, filing in Buffalo, tending the grounds of a nursing home in Abilene and what comes over me is not despair but absolute blankness.

— Christian Wiman, from *Filthy Lucre*

The ocean makes me a ruthlessly practical machine of self-repression. On the ocean I can simply blank out whole categories of feelings because they contribute nothing to the ongoing voyage. I'm a survivor. I travel light.

— Miles Hordern, from *Sailing the Pacific*

Fueling at the Pilot on Steele St., Denver, CO

Remembrance sweet routines early morning a thousand rituals tens of
thousands of times trailer hookup crank up the gear torque test the kingpin

important cold cab cold start turn the key press the ether button press the starter
hear that Detroit struggle start listen to the knock explode knock explode knock

start without spark wait for the warm-up wait for the heat see the breath know it
drive two blocks from terminal to truckstop steering pulling swing low swing wide

into any open bay insert the card magnetic strip up put on gloves fuel-stained
soaked unscrew the cap lift off the nozzle place in tank squeeze the handle

lock it on hear and smell the green gush release the rubber strap that secures the
driver side of the hood walk around the front undo the strap on the passenger side lift nozzle

at the satellite pump unscrew the cap so dirty so covered with diesel road grime oily dirt
grasp the pump nozzle by the right gloved hand grey leather blackened suede worn

shiny on fingers diesel raw fuel pouring rush gallon gush smell twin-stacked exhaust fills
lungs wakes me the jolt up ritual two-thirty Ogallala North Platte or Casper maybe a 4 a.m.

Ft. Morgan Sterling or nine o'clock at night blizzard early run to Durango Grand
Junction always dark always night morning or night sky black lit urban glow

point A to point B moon shining on fields of snow running lights brake lights
from truck trailers or cars then pull off my left-hand glove brace my left foot

on the fender pull down the great red hood pull the radiator grill toward me and down
tilt it up grab the short-handled sponge rubber blade near the pump climb use

the mirror bracket to pull up stand on the steer tire scrub down insects or snow debris
wet the windshield first few swipes wet the glass to soften sponge scrub scrub

squeegee off the excess line by line know this is your view clean it lower hood
back down use body to counterweight clean headlights for brightness for distance

to see and be seen rehook straps replace squeegee open the door grab the metal claw
hammer rests wedged between air-ride seat and a small extinguisher bracketed home

take this hammer thump sixteen tires walk the trailer make sure nothing hangs
unsecured recognize smile at the toll of springs bounce rubbing jolts knock vibration

heavy moving parts you command rub ill-secured hoses wires lines weight
that tears a road up finally the road will tear back with vengeance pocked salted

grooved by weight test those tires hold their pressure the thump the bounce
so gratifying hear feel it vibrate through that hammer handle check lights look

watch for DOT compliance write-ups related vaguely to safety walk the walk think
about the day about to begin mentally gear up run through the drops anticipate

difficulties bound to crop up to be faced head-on go back over that dream
you woke from remember only fragments strange but what the yes and you walk thump

thump past drivers past trailer tandems you walk lights lit thump thump a rhythm
feel good the world answers back to your knock you here it there thump thump

try to step over pools of diesel try not to get it on your shoes the smell in the cab
recall a close call some would white your hair some that barb-snagged you

top off satellite first both tanks 250 gallons in five minutes a hundred and fifty miles
five hundred miles or eight hundred miles a day you fill up whether needed or not

take on fuel for free coffee — you need that comfort your coffee like fueling
that warmth a buffer a movement a safety to face whatever waits

the small four-wheelers swerving to slide under the trailer the metal crescendo
forty cars piling up just inside the fog bank on either side of I-25 northbound southbound

the brake on black ice you know better knew better too late back through relentless snow
chains rollovers leaping deer spinouts jackknifes sleet sticking to the windshield

despite the heat the defrost the wipers gelling fuel Rocky Mountain subzero
windchill Wyoming wind gusts crossing conspiring to blow that trailer off the road

blast it on its side all of this and more to haul twenty tons of freight or pull a cubed-out
lighter trailer billboard exchange time of your life for money honor monkey reward

or shame clock-ticking world wheel-turning commerce trade economy rolling
rolling on into unseeable future marked by routine tedium of the dark day after day

even now I wash up still there still thinking of it doing it wee hours a dream
that won't end or be wakened from and I die they die in stained shards

in fiberglass fragments a cacophony of freezing fluids so brittle so messy so
over and over

Back to back runs in the Rockies

Sunflower seeds work best—
never knew whether by some property
or the act of splitting and spitting
the halves out. Cracking or lowering the window
helps, especially when cold or freezing.
Coffee, cigarettes help, but not really.
Loud music—jumping blues/rockabilly the best,
or books or sermons on tape, but these
only reveal how much you miss, and
thinking is the last thing you want to do.
Icy roads, blizzards (except for the soft
fluffy flakes that come at you like somnolent galaxies),
or screaming wind which rocks or pushes the trailer
all over the road is good—soft rain and swishing
wipers bad. Hard rain that makes it hard to see
is okay. Lots of curves or traffic help
but are no guarantee—

Driving too fast for conditions helps, sometimes
not. And of course the old standby, slapping your
face, hard, repeatedly. And if you really have to,
stopping the truck to get rid of the coffee,
then lapping the rig once or
twice, again, most effective in subzero.
Then there's periodic screaming to get the blood
going, talking to oneself—bouncing in the air-
ride seat to music—if absolutely all else fails—as last
resort (since this can be dangerous)—a "ten-minute nap"
over the wheel, on the shoulder, close to the road—
(leave radio on—squelch up high).
If you oversleep, soon enough, you want to hear the
roar of the truck going by and reel with the wind
of his passing, or hear him holler an offer for aid,
in case you might need it. Which you would, to wake you,
not because you're broke down.

Hallucinations mean it's time to stop—proceed at
own risk—trucks jackknifing up to a "door," at you
doing sixty, or leaping or crawling shadows across the road
mean shut down to any wise person, but I usually
wouldn't—Sleep, the Enemy—at long last
the welcomest friend.

Meeting

. . . and will pursue his enemies into darkness

– from *Nahum* 1:8

I didn't need to but wanted to stop, rolling off I-10 to the rest area, just so I could take a closer look at the rocks, the cactus, and air. A Navajo in state khakis is cleaning and restocking the restrooms, his storage closet is open, mop and bucket out. It's moving on toward twilight already and the reddish landscape shimmers an even more orange shade that can haunt dreams. Heat dies down emanating from the ground more than the washed-out sky of burnished blue. What I really want is water and have my jug ready. Before I say a word, the Navajo knows what I'm looking for, so he points to a faucet jutting out from the building where he fills his mop bucket, and missing a handle, he gets out a key to work it open for me while I hold the jug under and water pours out. More than water I just want to watch him work to learn something of his life. We talk a moment and he says something memory hides, refuses to call back.

Untamed and terrible, the desert stretches flat and far to the south, dipping down into Mexico. To the north, an outcropping of sandstone and boulders stands before me. The highway points inevitably fixed east and west through this terrifying, vast expanse inhabited by ghosts. Saguaro are the closest thing to human out there. Life is just on the verge of rising to meet the dark and I pause to look around so as to absorb the scene like some faulty camera before hopping back into the idling cool of my fiberglass cab. This pulls a baking aluminum box which is the sole purpose for me being here. Release the brake with the heel of my hand, check mirrors, push in clutch and shift then begin to roll and run through the gears. A few hours from Phoenix with 46,000 pounds of pasta, outrunning something in the coming dark. Commence passing or be passed up the line, coming headlights are glowing eyes lighting downstream while up ahead are red tails in the hallelujah night. Window down air hot over a thrum of moving wheels which sing to me across asphalt in a rumble of wind pushed by motoring engines. I am truly alone but there seems to be a world crashing against me out in the dark. In dreams I can never find Arizona — lost, hidden, missing from every atlas and signpost. I don't know why.

CB Conversation #3: Flying J Truckstop, North Platte, NE— The I-80 Closure from Pine Bluffs to Rawlins for 36 Hours

"Is the road open yet or still closed."

"I got a number for Wyoming road conditions —
just called them an hour ago —
road'll be shut down till tomorrow morning.
The truckstop at Big Springs is full up
and you won't get no farther tonight."

"Copy that — okeedokee — I got fifty bucks
for anyone willing to move, so I can park.

"Damn, if the fool knew how to park,
he could keep his fifty bucks — there's
still parking driver, if you can blind back
a rig —"

"Fifty bucks to show me how it's done mister —
you don't know where I been, how long I been up,
or what I drove through to get here!"

"There's five inches of hail in this parking lot —"
"Eastbound. . . . Is the road open or closed?"

"Rollovers, jackknifes — nobody's going anywhere!"

"There's gotta be a highway around this interstate!"

Two-lanes are closed too, driver . . ."

"Anybody need pallets? I got 4X4s to sell.
Go to twenty-two."

". . . I had mirrors installed on the ceiling. I got sheer curtains
on the windows. I'm sittin' here wearing nothing but a silk
kimono, with my feet up, drinking a rum and coke."

"Where you at, Ladybug — if you look anything like
you sound, I'd like to meet you."

"She's probably twelve years old, and got your number."

"I'm twenty-eight, five foot eight, and a hundred and fifteen pounds —
my voice isn't half as sexy as I am."

"Well damn! This is Icecream Cone — where you at?"

"I'm in the back row, just like you.
 It wouldn't be half as fun if I told you exactly where—
 I'm just talking trash to pass the time. You know, even
 stuck in a snowstorm outside Wyoming isn't half
 as bad as the job in the real world I used to have.
 I'll be here a day, then I'm gone—every morning,
 something different."

"Hey how 'bout a burger or cup of coffee with ol'
 Icecream Cone—you don't have to worry about me—I'm
 in my fifties—I just wanna chat. . . ."

"Shit, anybody know if 76 is open? I gotta be in Salty
 in the morning—I'll cut across the Rockies if I have to.
 Eastbound?"

"Driver—last I heard 70 was open,
 but the chain law's in effect for single-screws
 over Eisenhower and Vail. You should be
 able to get over it and be there in less than twelve hours,
 but it's slow going, and pretty shitty though."

"Yeah, but is 80 open to 76
 and 76 open to Denver . . . eastbound!"

"Icecream Cone, she's all talk—
 you want some real company?
 Go to 15 . . ."

"Mayflower—hold up—you'll never get it
 that way—let me get my shoes on. I'll guide you back."

" —don't really want to get out of the truck in just a kimono . . ."

"Where's that Ladybug at? I've looked at every truck
 in the back row and I don't see you."

"Hey, I'm here—the third truck from the end."

"Dayaamn, but she got her a voice, ain't she—whooowhee!"

"You next to that May truck?"

"No—but I'm back here."

"How 'bout that cup of coffee, Ladybug?
 I won't bite or take advantage."

"I can't. I'm married.

My husband's asleep in the bunk."

"You bitch! I've been listening to you flirt
 with these guys for hours, and then we
 find out you're married, and you don't
 want to finish what you started.
 You're probably a three-hundred-pound sow
 and uglier than a slab of pork belly — if
 your husband were to catch you talking
 this shit and leading drivers on the way you have
 he'd kick your butt so hard
 you'd be doing somersaults out of the cab!"

"Break one nine — is the road open or closed?
 Can I get a straight answer?"

"Driver — go up to 25 —
 I'll give you some phone numbers to call."

"42 — on my way."

"What do you know about my marriage!
 I never see my husband, except
 as we're crawling past each other
 from bunk to steering wheel."

"Why aren't you in there with him now then,
 instead of bullshitting other poor lonely drivers —
 probably because you're so butt ugly!"

"Ooooh! That lady mean — she so mean
 when she die the worms'll be eating
 her face and look up at each other
 and say, 'oooh, don't she taste mean!' "

"My company keeps us rolling — this rig's wheels turn nonstop,
 except for road closures and to load or unload —
 my husband's dead tired. I'm not bad looking,
 but the only time I feel pretty is among truckers!"

"Well. What's your excuse, honey? Why
 aren't you tired, or are you one of them
 sleeper-team partners that only books time
 and lets her husband do all the work?"

"Now now ladies . . ."
"Anybody interested in a Cobra radio or a birddog —

go to 22—I'm practically giving them away."

"Bitch! How'd you . . ."

"That driver's gonna hit—Schneider—look out!
Aw Geez."

"Where are . . ."

"My marriage is pretty good, I guess."

". . . just can't hack it . . . praise the open road . . . hate the life . . ."

"Look at that schmuck in front of the US Express truck—"
Laughter.
"He be out in the wind and sleet dinkin' around with his satellite
dish for over a half hour, while his co-driver be movin' her hand
this way and that inside the cab in her underwear."

"Oh man—I just want to know the road conditions. . . ."

"Everybody's get . . . stepped on."

"You're the ugly . . ."

"Hot air melt this snow."

"Copy that."

". . . I drive . . . US Express . . . come on."

"Go to 32, roger?"

"Whew boy—what started all this—

just turned my radio on. Too much estrogen
in my radio! Yeoow! What's with them two?"

"Why don't you come over and . . ."

"Fuckin' weather, fuckin' roads and fuckin' truckstops!"

"Oooh mama, copy that—cat scratch fever!"

"Ah for Christ's sake! No place to park, and fuckin' drivers screaming at each other—shit!
Get the hell outta my radio!"

CB Conversation #2: The Siren Call in Winnemucca, NV

"Drivers, how about a free shower,
  coffee and some conversation—"

"She means the universal language—"

"We love truckers.
 We have fifteen girls here . . .
 different nationalities—
 infinite variety,
 and showers are free—"

"Will y'all scrub my back for free?"

"No, hand, but those showers are mandatory—
 they make you take one
 whether you need one or not—"

"Chances are you need one, roger?"

"Well, how'd you like to lay with a stinky
 trucker—think about it"

"Hey, I resemble that remark!"

"I had my weekly shower yesterday—
 it's Saturday, ain't it?"

"Drivers come on out for some
 coffee and conversation—
 we got us a little strip joint,
 some dancers who take it **all off**,
 who want to party and have some fun—
 come back—
 we can send some girls out to pick you up.
 We take checks and major credit cards—
 but remember the showers and coffee
 are free—come out for some conversation.
 We look forward to it!"

CB Conversation #4: from Walker Lake to Hawthorne, NV— Two Drivers Discuss the Birds and the Bees

"Yeah, there was this girl
 working behind a desk at my terminal—
 I mean drop-dead gorgeous,
 blonde hair, looked like Morgan Fairchild,
 come on.

"I asked her out—she said, 'I'm gay.'
 I said, 'What?'
 She said, 'I'm lesbian—
 I'm off men—don't have nothin'
 to do with 'em . . .'
 I said, 'That's funny, I'm a lesbian, too.'
 She looked at me funny, said, 'What?'
 I said, 'I'm a lesbian trapped in a man's body,'
 come on."

Laughs into the mic, "Roger that I do.
 I dated this girl for a while.
 I thought we were really going somewhere,
 then one day we're at this high-end restaurant,
 eating stuffed portobello mushrooms
 for an appetizer, you know—
 she'd been kind of quiet the whole night,
 so I knew something was up—then she dropped it:
 she said, 'I really like you a lot,
 but there's something you need to know—
 I'm bisexual.' Shit!"

"You know I don't think I'd have
 any problem with that! I would not
 have any problem with that—If I'd caught
 my ex-wife with another woman,
 I'd have said, 'That's alright, baby,
 knock yourself out! Have some fun!'
 Come back."

"Yeah, I was tempted to ask her
 to invite her friend over
 but it was kind of a shock."

"You know, I gotta tell you something:
 Since I been divorced, all of a sudden,
 I got more money than I know what

69

to do with—my oldest is twenty—she was
shacking up with this Mexican kid—well,
actually he's not a kid—he's thirty-five
and she's twenty—

"I told her, 'Honey, you gotta find yourself
someone with a car and a job—someone
who can take care of you.' She didn't listen.
Two years later, she calls me up—'Dad,
can I stay at your place for a while?'
I said, 'You left the house two years ago,
and you haven't talked to me since—
now you want to come back home?'
Come to find out the Mexican kid's in jail,
and she's got a baby.
I said, 'Didn't I tell you the Mexican kid
was no good for you?'
She said, 'Yes.'
I said, 'Didn't I tell you you'd ruin
your life with this guy?'
She said, 'Yes.'
I said, 'You've ruined your life—
just ruined your life,
and now you've got a baby.'
She said, 'Yes.'
I said, 'If it wasn't for that baby
there's no way in hell you'd
come back to live in my house—'
I know for a fact she isn't welcome
at her mother's house—
she's living with my best friend.
Grass is always greener, come on."

"I hear that—roger on the more money—
I'm paying child support to my ex,
but I still have more than I've ever seen—
look out. We got us a bear on the side over here
fixin' to shoot us in the back—"

"Copy that!
What's the speed limit through here,
come on?"

"Forty-five I think—haven't seen any other signs . . ."

"Aye four."

Flowers or toilet paper

o what a proud dreamhorse moving(whose feet
almost walk air).

— ee cummings, from **"what a proud dreamhorse"**

From the Georgia Pacific paper mill in Halsey, OR,
to Costcos in Albuquerque, NM, I haul my load.
I missed the 191 and find myself in Grand Junction;
to get back on route I must cut down through Ouray
and over Red Mountain Pass to Durango.
Gorgeous scenery, yes, but after chaining up, I must negotiate
a fourteen-foot-high trailer though a rough-hewn hole in rock
the sign says is 13'9", pull my twenty thousand pounds
of toilet paper and paper towels over cinder-strewn packed powder
up ten mph switchbacks and, in the space of a mile, pass signs
warning of avalanche, falling rock, deer and elk and 6–7% grades,
repeatedly. There is no shoulder or guardrail and the cliffs
are sheer, and as I ponder these things, I also
wonder will the dear people of Albuquerque, Costco
bargain shoppers all, think of me as they mop spills
or wipe their asses with sheet after sheet from the reams
I bring them from afar — I am paid to do this.

Half my trailer goes to the first Costco at 3 a.m. my time.
I make it. Glory.
While I wait for the receiver to check
in the load with a handheld device that registers bar codes
and marvel at the finesse of the forklift driver
stacking and maneuvering pallets on a loading dock
too small,
an impatient man appears — a straight-truck
driver — he opens his door, and there
perishable beauty is rolled out on racks
onto the concrete floor; flamboyant colors ridiculous
surfeit in variety. A multitude, meticulously grown, cut, wrapped,
the names of which, surely as marvelous and Latinate,
I, being rude and unschooled, can not possibly be expected to guess or know.
Placed in buckets rolled out before the indifferent eyes of the receiver,
checking boxes off on the load manifest — flowers
don't come with bar codes — I ask myself
which load is more worthy more necessary,
more equitable, should a life be risked to deliver it? — done,

he reloads the racks, takes the buckets, some empty now,
and throws the water in them forward onto the wooden bed
of his truck to wash the floor clean.

Invincible

We form a funeral procession
first the right then the left slows
passing, studying
to pay respects
without eulogy, but the turnout staggers
the honor
the spotlight enviable
as I gaze and nod and pass.
First, feeling relieved
for myself for not being directly involved —
followed by the unnameable, unutterable
sadness for him . . .
lastly, I'm pissed — LA morning traffic!

But when he woke this morning
what myriad mélange of tasks, desires, plans,
what future occupied him — what adrenaline exaltation —
did he dream
of sudden dying;
no.

Would he be brokering some big business deal,
late to high school, college,
work? And was there promise,
or none at all, and this the outcome
anyone who knew him might expect,
or worse?

First, the yellow Ducati laid in speed skidded
on its side,
little dents, liquid leaks, body behind,
cocooned, ageless, crumpled
face ciphered by helmet
— yellow bike with matching helmet and custom leather suit
means money, meaning recklessness
not desperation not — body somehow shrunken,
smaller in death,
no blood no gore lying ignored, unattended
all help too late
lying there, still, by the police
interviewing witnesses more important now; somewhere out there an
ambulance transport to the morgue is unable to bypass gridlock.

Us, the mourners the living, skirt the dumb thing what once
was a bounded universe—a dynamo of movement and symbiosis
attended by such biological machinations so much more than,
hands and feet deleted, systems the product some say
of infinite mind, joyriding like Hermes,
these winged feet a late technology of fast wheels turning,
not quite capable of flight—

Surely the light of consciousness must beat out the rest?
Wishing to get around, get on, see and feel, but leaving
left just so much plastic metal and yellow-clad meat.

Ourselves witnesses feeling whatever it is we feel:
pity, contempt, awe, perhaps only annoyance—how do we not
read in this
letters of a sign, and our exit?

Ode to G.D. Winter and his Peterbilt, #08, Out of Bates, MO

His tractor is the color of cream soda. The trailer
is blemishless, split tandems and shiny aluminum
hubs, sides lined with corrugated panels of gleaming
stainless steel with chrome trim which never
rubbed a pole, brushed a tree branch, or haplessly
backed into any other rig or obstacle — nothing ever
touches this rig but his foot on the step and throttle,
bumpers, dockplates, and the buffing chamois,
though the Pete's stretched out wheelbase
must be enormous — even rocks and road
grime must veer away in the reflected light
from the great, antique machine.
The headlamps and trailer lights sport little hoods like visors.
The Thermo King panels shine brilliantly in the sun.
A rising swan rests over the big square hood
with 550 horses underneath, the air horn
sounds like a freight train's, twin chrome
stacks and air dryers ride on either side,
along with scores of yellow marker lights
the length of the rig.

Mr. Winter shows off the truck to his son,
whose smile never leaves his face — he sits
behind the wheel to glimpse what his father sees —
certainly only a fraction of the stories have been told
from an era now diminishing — as I sit in the ugly,
scarred, but newer truck next to him, I recount to myself the meaner,
shorter history of tight docks, narrow misses. And not so missed.
The rude drivers and bad weather during the countless miles
freight got delivered during my driving career,
longing for the memories he might share —
the decades of joys and shame,
encountered through melting dusks and dawns
next to broken lines like seconds to a mile's
minute, along two-lanes and interstates. Finally,
no longer able to restrain the desire to talk to this journeyman,
like some medieval warrior in ancient armor,
but without one visible battle scar — his son had come and gone —
I stepped out of my truck and rapped
gently on his door while he sat
catching up his log before the next trip.

"Beautiful rig," I said, "what year is it?"
"It's a 2000." He reads and answers

the astonishment in my face with a wry smile.
"This is my fifteenth truck in forty-five years of driving—
I spec them out, then take them to auction
at Sioux City. Some young buck always buys them.
This one has all sorts of toys and goodies
and I'll be turning it in soon . . . it has 165,000 on it,
and I'd like to put another hundred thousand on,
but my wife's after me to hang it up. I'm sixty-five,
and she's been putting up with me for forty-two years,
and only now is she raising hell for me to retire."

"Do you think you can really give it up?" I asked.
"Don't you think as soon as you've gotten home,
your wife'll be asking when you're heading
out again?" His grin shows gaps and gold.
He pulls out an unfiltered cigarette, but doesn't light it.

"I live here in St. Joe, and stop off at the house
once a week—I run the South to the Northwest.
On my way to Seattle now—I think my wife is right.
It's time to have some fun." He looks doubtful,
and since I don't know him it's hard to tell if the doubt
is due to health, or the prospect of fun without work.

He asks about my company and how I like it—
where I'm headed and where I came out of—I tell him this.
He praises my company and seems pleased
I didn't bitch or tear it down—
he has friends that drive for them. Of course.

"In order for an owner operator to make it these days
you have to get in with someone and be loyal—
I waited five days down in Florida for a load of tomatoes—
you've got to be loyal—and attentive. The most
important thing for a driver to be is attentive. So many
kids these days are cowboys."

I have no idea what he means
by "attentive," but at least I recognize this
as the nugget I came for.

"Well, I'm off to Seattle—how was the weather, son?"

I tell him about the snow when I came through.

"Well, my chains are ready!"

"You're getting a little old to be hanging iron, aren't you?"

75

"I've done it for years—I don't have any problems."

His tanned and weathered face and thin build don't deny this.
He lights the smoke, smiles, and waves just before he
presses the ignition—the sound deep and sweet.
"Remember, son—be attentive."

I turn back to my battered Freightliner,
the white fiberglass hood smeared with bugs,
the badge of sand from a snowy pass
thousands of miles away—
the Thermo King panels globbed with grease,
the trailer marked by inattention.
I know this is there but don't really see it,
because my eyes are still dazzled by chrome.

Trailer 2542L

There are things you find nothing about in books.

– Joseph Conrad, from *Typhoon*

In the beginning it only cost a few drivers
their jobs, before word got out, and the liability
became expensive in other ways. It started out

mildly; a disputable thing. The queer frequency
of mundane mechanical failures — lights that lit
or didn't; lug nuts flying off wheels bounced into

people's windshields; tires throwing tread; brakes that locked
up without apparent reason, on ice or in a heavy downpour
when the trailer was empty . . . air lines leaked or gladhands

refused to seal — routine failures plaguing especially if poorly
serviced by the mechanic, or pre-trips were not
properly conducted. Murphy's Law covered a multitude

of sins, but eventually drivers detected a pattern, started
talking, and dreaded seeing 2542 on a load manifest. Footsteps
up and down the aluminum length, which started

up after the exhausted driver crashed in the sleeper
for some badly needed shuteye. Later, overweight
fines at the weigh station after the load had been scaled

and checked after loading and the axle spread had been correct.
Not all that unusual; loads can sometimes shift if poorly braced.
Driver error, the company thought. Trailers are such

expensive pieces of equipment, the company
was far too large and too slow to take notice, but
began to, after injuries kept cropping up associated

with this particular trailer: a driver's wrist
was broken by yanking on a stubborn handle to adjust
the tandems that released too suddenly; another got

a broken jaw from a landing gear crank; a roll
of carpet crushed an ankle; a wardrobe fell
on a driver inexplicably during a furniture

delivery; a back went out; a finger sliced badly;
a dockworker was run over by a seasoned forklift
operator loading 2542L. Mechanics at various terminals

laughed at the bitch sheets that rolled in with this trailer, after
almost every load. They began to anticipate,
track, place bets. Writing ran down the walls inside, words

revealed some little insult or embarrassment
personally directed at the reader; or mere
curses in graffiti taken to be gibberish;

dents, scarrings or strange markings appeared and disappeared
on the outside. Mists, smells, ignis fatuus; sounds of singing
in the dark recesses of the nose made warehouse crews

wary—hostlers flat-out refused to pick the thing up
or move it. Freight rearranged itself; multiple drops within
shrink-wrapped pallets got mixed up inside of a thousand

miles and sealed doors—the shipper swore up and down it had
been picked and loaded correctly. Jinxed trailer—gremlins—
haunted trailer. Finally, even the higher-ups fed up,

cognizant, and grappling bravely with this not
merely empirical problem, schemed to have the decals
stripped, the thing auctioned off. They assigned the trailer

to a top driver to bring home one last load bound for the base
terminal in Missoula: some ex-military company man, a
Viet Cong-killing supertrucker who scoffed

at the stories and superstition. He pulled it close
to two thousand miles without hitch from Newark. . . .
While perhaps it might be more satisfying to end this story

with a dramatic denouement, something like this:
"For their final act, he pulled into a truckstop in Spearfish,
began backing into a slot next to a placarded

tanker when the fifth wheel disengaged from the kingpin.
Aluminum is such flammable metal—might have been
magnesium to judge by the flare. The story makes

the national papers. At the nearby fuel island,
a reefer trailer's Thermo King stops holding
the programmed temp even though the color-coded light

lies green, but blowing heat instead of frigid air. The load
is lost, but the driver only loses his job . . ." Problem is,
this would be the stuff of a 19th century Joseph Conrad tale,

wouldn't it? Truth is, he pulled into the Missoula yard
with the damned thing! I know nothing after that.
I never heard another word from anyone about it.

Piss Bottle

They appear to me worse than any dark prophecy, these discarded, big-neck bottled ambers, never noticed before but everywhere now, scat liquid containers flung from heavy-hauler windows which roll to rest on wide interstate shoulders, or standing in empty slots of truckstop tarmac for someone else to run over, abandoned beside fence lines, or the edges of wide-turn accessible big-box parking lots. Relieved to be rid, they shout to me thus: rude contempt, harried pressure, lazy shame, the toll of work and bitterness, a type of man, bodily process, a hasty journey not half done (underneath all, the thought: never enough . . .), a wasted drink deposit, its lid screwed tight on what's ripening to darker brown in the sun.

Thankful

Black scars scab the road with rubber —
disjointed, and unnaturally, skids
that unintended crisis braking
litters of glitter, windshield diamond glass
crunch under tires like dark-theater popcorn.

On cue less than a mile further, the wrecker
hooks on to a loggers' fork dolly —
tractor absent — logs if there ever were any,
and victim also hauled off soonest,
most liable to need.

All that remains: aftermath —
the usual sad suspects — darkened
puddle of sudden blood or oil. Except this:
two miles later, just outside town,
at the out-of-service service station

between pumps and passenger side
of his rig — hidden almost — he stands
motioning at the cab door like
a log truck driver distraught, arms shaking
outstretched in exhortation, prayer, or exorcism.

On the driver's side door most visible
by backward look was painted large-lettered
and cursive, "*THANKFUL*."

Dusk on I-15, Between Butte and Helena, MT

For lack of a pistol, a hammer'd have to do —
the small straggler hesitated, doubled back, and
jake brake, empty trailer, hard brake, and the swerve all
failed to save the fawn — fender clipped and snapped its back —
I almost thought I missed it for any impact
I felt. But then, damn it, over the CB, "Hey
Shepard, that fawn you hit ain't dead — it's flopping in
the road." I could've kept going, but couldn't. Not exactly
flopping, but lying in the middle of the interstate,
head up looking around as though in a meadow

surrounded by flowers. For a minute, I hoped
I'd only stunned the deer and it'd scrabble away on
shaky hooves. I slid it from road to shoulder, cussing,
it watching, all trusting, with those blank, big eyes, as
though I might help. An Albertson's driver pulled over
and stepped out of his cab — "Got a gun?" I asked. "Nope."
He walked over and kicked the hind legs, "Shit, back's broke.
Only one way out of this for her." He scanned the
horizon for the herd; why, I could only guess.
"Yeah," I said, looking down, patting its bony head,
tugging the ears gently. "You mind doing it?" He

looked up then, frowned, shook his head, then held out a hand
for the hammer — stood behind, so it wouldn't see it
coming, came down with a crack, too lightly, I thought,
hit square with the sideways flat of the head. The fawn's
head hovered a second, then, as if remembering,
sank with a groan and gush of breath. "You sure it's dead?"
I wanted to hit it again just to make sure,
imagining its head popping up again, bleating — one
mercy killing was more than I could stomach.
"You hear that noise she made? Skull's real thin on top — she's

dead all right." For a long time later I still wondered,
wished I'd have made sure. Sometimes still do — imagine
it lying there, in the night, suffering, but quietly,
as only animals do, forsaken by herd,
waiting for coyotes to come make sense of its death.

Homage to 'Roy Jones

He told stories as we loaded my freight,
nicknamed me "the snowman."
When he pulled tankers over Loveland
"You never needed to hang iron," he said
(I was forever changing out my chains' broken
cross links), "because the highway was gravel
and the trannies then were geared so low

you could pull the pass in first
and never spin a wheel." Now, working
in a warehouse at seventy-five, he talked of retiring—
first it was St. Augustine, but later
Toronto, as soon as he could afford it.
"Another year," he'd say. He still grieved for
his wife, fifteen years his junior, who left

him, keeping his car and house,
when the cyst on his forehead turned out
to be malignant, and the radiation made
him "hard to live with," he'd tell me,
then bitterly, "Gotta go burn one."
He'd dolly the furniture across miles of concrete
floor, from railcar to trailer gingerly,

slow, steady, as though it hurt to walk,
but, arms strong, could empty a boxcar
right along with the lazy twenty-year-olds.
"Damn, Leroy," I asked him one day,
"Why'd you hang it up—a bad wreck?"
I never could fathom working twice as hard
for a fraction the pay, especially at his age.

"Nope. Drove for thirty years and I've seen it
all, boy. I just woke up one morning
in a rest area—my face as pale as yours—I
was pulling a parking lot, and was halfway to my drop
cross country—I just couldn't do it.
Couldn't do it anymore.
Called the man, told him to come

pick up his truck, the keys'd be in it.
Sometimes for a while after I'd go
sit at the bus station to breathe
in the sweet diesel exhaust—it's addicting—
you wait and see, that's what you gonna do
after you had enough." I laughed,
shook my head, not understanding, then.

The Jolly Season in Steamboat Springs

Christmas nears, company coming — living room must be set — showed off.
This high-end ski town, downtown, looks snatched from the sky — from the book
of Revelation after Armageddon — streets of icy gold. Trees drip lights and frost
and every shop window frames twinkling warmth, smells waft of burning fir and steamy
cidery cheer. The sight and contrast of light and warmth like heaven, doors dead-bolted,
alarmed. Gritty from rolling under the rig, my hair drips, eyes tear, wet with the cold.

On the phone they said, "Spend the night." I told them "No way." They didn't hear me
laugh, how loudly but inside, when, "Our help will meet you — call when you get in."
They, the tucked-in affluent, jammied, or under comforter making mad love — whatever;
proud business owner in a high-end heaven town. Late, downy parka-clad romance still strolls by,
lovers so romantic, ah — dreaming — I, the exile, had spun out on Toponas Pass,
a narrow strip, managed to back it off into the berm to chain — mini-flash between

my teeth. Two four-wheelers, nervous — one spun out next to my left — wouldn't meet
my eyes when I offered aid, apologies, or a tow. "Jeep got four-wheel drive?" "Broken!"
she replied, stared straight ahead — pissed, scared? Boyfriend walked back. I brushed off
sopping coveralls, kicked off my feet on the step before I climbed back
into the cab, pulled out, chained to the teeth. She can blame me — my truck is always
in the way. That's my job, lady. Ho ho hoed, under my breath. Damn good thing I'd

spun out too. Visibility for shit — oncoming four-wheelers pushed my rig out past the fog line,
headlights glaring, they'd left Steamboat hugging the centerline because drifts
obscured the road; dark heavy snow over ice forced my need for every bit of traction.
After double parking, I slide the cartons and several-thousand-dollar sofas
off the back end of the trailer to the hippie kid who ganders my damp coveralls
and the accretion of snow and ice melting off the truck, while the temp climbs, flurries slow.

What's stuck to the side and undercarriage heavier than the freight I hauled in.
He smiles, says, "Some shit, huh?" Then gives his dreads a shake as if to say,
"Going over Rabbit Ears tonight, man?" He whistles — points at the chains, gives me
the thumbs up — "Dude." "Dude," I say. We wave each the other off. Shops glow, unearthly.
Before I race the hill to skim over icy patches the cindery snowplow missed, and anxiously eye
the lurching rpm gauge, maybe spin out chained-but-stalled on the slick pass, or,

just slowly wend my way back through the wilderness hours, nothing but jumping blues
for company back over Loveland, coasting so cautious down into my dirty dingy white town,
I decide I must linger longer in Heaven, carefully catalog each sight and sound,
smell every smell, revel in cold and wet seeping through insulated coveralls, with just
that hint of warmth and scent passing through the glass of each shop window I walk past,
glazed and glaring with all the richness, mulled spices, the life of that world inside.

The Hauling Witness

Slid past now some pretty cities lit casinoed struck rich, but what once were
poverished pockets of old mountain mining towns, risen. Bouncing glint
of moon or stars they lie, hide, rest or ridden, askance steel rails hard
grey blue or black in black of night, but this one snowlit lighter
a buzz glisten beam vibrate with coming headlight pushing, pulling,
car houses of metal housing freight over ice shines a sound, quick
pulses like a feeling steel cold through this Colorado canyon cutting
across state along river, Glenwood now, from up beyond upscale ski towns
dollared snow Vail passes pines interstate by ways of tunnels, several,
through mountains, rocks, over tracks ties snowfalls fine powdery fluff
flaky quarters, amassed, a whistle pours, screech of wheels on rails cornering
and whine engines a roar of grate and shine on over through to Junction,
then honeyed sunrise behind driving beyond toward a blood-rocked sky
setting west amid fuel fumed and exhausted grease, smoke huff steam thaw

Denver

Branches clack and chime armored in ice, lit
by soft, cold lamps above our heads. Branches
could crack under too much wind, but what a
walk it makes as we watch our breath and gaze

down the crunchy, snowpacked street at night, in
love, talking of futures. On this brittle,
late white night, we walk between dark windows,
a block from our brick Victorian. Sounds

of shots, trains, and barks of dogs shushed by snow
and highway noise lull us to sleep after
hot, hushed love in bed (not wishing to wake
the futures which lie asleep close by). Too

few hours later I must get up, grab truck-
stop coffee, drive the treacherous mountains.

[We the despoilers, the bloodthirsty, corrupt, a few days before Christmas]

Highway 97 runs through the high desert town of Madras, a one-way on either side through the downtown core. White holiday lights decorate the trees that line shopfronts and sidewalk. In an empty dirt lot between buildings is a square filled with standing cut pine trees for sale, framed by a tabernacle of strung lighting which says, open for business. But no one is stopping. The dime-store lights open to sky burn so much lesser than the stars they mirror but great too: two different kinds of makers each according to its kind. To one side is a small camp trailer, and a burn barrel with flame blazing brightly and warm; out of the barrel comes the color of fall maples, heat and motion dying alive, like glowing bronze arms and hands that reach up and out. Two attendants, long bored with each other and the night, stand near the fire for warmth, wishing either for customers or clock hands to push the evening closed, anxious to get on with the evening. Nearly everyone has already bought and placed their trees in special rooms or corners of their homes — transfiguring the cut green life into shining little purveyors of scent and light and color. Semi and car traffic drives through town from somewhere on their way to somewhere else. The army of the Lord appeared singing peace to such as these.

Notes on Poems

The title of this book is a nod toward Linda Greenlaw's *Seaworthy*, her bestselling sequel to *The Hungry Ocean*. Both are memoirs detailing adventures of a swordboat captain fishing in the Grand Banks of the Atlantic for swordfish and lobsters. It's no big stretch to compare small commercial fishing boats with long-haul trucking. I'd say the stakes and risks involved in both professions are separated by relative levels of magnitude. While hers seems way more dangerous to me, the liability and perils of commercial driving can be risky and comparable in interesting ways, as partially outlined in these pages.

No Pirate, No Cowboy But Very Blue Collar, at the Dollar Tree in Eastport Plaza, Portland, OR: Regarding this title—truck drivers often affect costumes and personas as a part of their job, perhaps unsurprisingly, considering the somewhat wandering, lonely, disreputable, and outlaw nature of the profession which nonetheless involves sacrifice, commitment and fatiguing, and often relentless, tediously difficult work. Part of it is a serious romanticism of work, eccentricity, and a loner-misfit mentality and partly—perhaps?—it is a gentle self-mockery or caricature. I'm not sure why they do this, and while not everyone does, it should be noted that there is a huge and diverse range of "types" within the industry across various ages, levels of education, and cultures of driver, whether short-line, regional or long-haul. The temperament required to drive long-haul and do it capably is peculiar, and not many are capable or equipped and few choose to do this for long. Many can do it for a while. The job is quite punishing to the body over time and many drivers die relatively young. For some reason the drivers that picked up the sea containers at port terminals that came over on barges from Asia were all Russian immigrants and they would no doubt laugh at this characterization because for them a truck is only a machine to be operated and a tool of capitalism or something they fell into because friends or relatives got them into it. Many owner operators in Seattle—running up and down the I-5 corridor—are Sikhs. However, for a while many eccentrically adopted the costumes and personas of either cowboy or pirate (varying from mild to outrageous); whether this was due to previous professions or origins, or the movies, I don't know, but from the mid-1990s to 2010 during my stint driving over-the-road it was common enough. My persona was more a uniform of T-shirt and shorts wearing a company ball cap kind of driver. It may surprise the reader to know as well that people go into trucking for many reasons and in my travels it was not uncommon to come across drivers with graduate degrees, on their second or third career like the retired airline pilot I knew, or another friend who drove in the winter and worked for the forestry department as a hydrologist in the summer, or husbands and wives who'd owned and sold businesses and now wanted to "see" the country together as sleeper-team drivers. Another thing I noticed over time was a distinct shift away from courtesy, manners, and professionalism, after driving in the nineties, leaving the life and then re-entering a truck cab over a decade later.

Huge Photograph of a Logging Crew Hung in Burger King, Near the Dollar Tree in White City, OR: While this is an ekphrastic poem, the Burger King located in White City is off the beaten path and just over ten miles east of I-5. After my delivery, I studied the photo carefully, scribbled a note about Rancheria Area 1938, and then later wrote the poem based on my memory of it. I tried to secure a copy of the photograph from the Oregon Historical Society photograph archives to compare the photo with the poem. The photo wasn't online and they were asking twenty dollars for an electronic copy, which was reasonable enough but at the time seemed too much, if I could not be positive I was actually buying the same photograph hanging in the store. Then, years later I drove out of my way to view the photo hanging in the Burger King. Not surprisingly, the details from memory were different from the actual photo, so some details from the poem do not match the photo. This is not a bad thing, but should be noted.

The two plates listing names on either side of the middle caption read as follows:

> Left Plate:
> Front Row: Ray Tungate, Anzel Conley, Charlie Page, Kenny Moore, Jeff Crumley, Bill Thomas, Bud Pope, Claude Baker, & Jess Rodgers.
>
> Center Plate:
> Rancheria Area 1938
> 9'4" Diam. Giant Sugar Pine
>
> Right Plate:
> Back Row: Ed Albern, Frank Smith, Albert Holm, Les Casey, & Lou Geppert.

a cougar's death on a blizzard-shadowed road: I-5 near Cottage Grove, mm 175 or so.

Smoke Break: The reference at the end of the poem to gamma-ray bursters comes from *Contact with Alien Civilizations: Our Hopes and Fears about Encountering Extraterrestrials*, Michael A. G. Michaud, page 108.

Train, Bird, Man, Behind the Dollar Tree in Milton, WA: Embedded is a reference to Hank Williams's song, "I'm So Lonesome I Could Cry" because of the train whistle and the bird. His lyric:

> *The moon just went behind the clouds*
> *To hide its face and cry*

Caught out of hours and regrettably handing off my rollers to Jim at the Dollar Tree in Beaverton, OR: "out of hours" refers to hours of service regulated by the DOT. Basically the law was that in any seven-day period a driver could work no more than sixty hours (or seventy hours in an eight-day period) total before having to take a thirty-four-hour break to reset and start over. Also, importantly, in a twenty-four-hour period, one could work up to fourteen hours and allowed to drive no more than eleven of the fourteen without first taking a ten-hour break to restart a new workday. You also were required to show a thirty-minute break after eight hours on duty. Depending on variable start and stop time in a given twenty-four hour period of one calendar day, this might cause some odd overlap of on-duty or off-duty but you were never legally capable of working (or logging) more than fourteen hours. For example: if your day (mid-night) started in the middle, you could drive six, go off-duty ten, and drive another seven and three-quarters, actually driving almost fourteen hours in a twenty-four-hour period. At the beginning of every driving period you had to log fifteen minutes for pre-trip/fueling and were required to log that thirty-minute break off duty, unless like the example above, your sleeper berth/off duty time acted as your break before eight hours of driving had transpired.

If you worked your fourteen hours per day you'd be out of hours in five days or less, and then need to take a thirty-four-hour break (a day and a half) before you could start working again. Sometimes this break fit nicely between one load and delivery and the next load, sometimes not, say if you had two long and expedited runs (hot loads) in a row. This rule was the main reason why most drivers falsified their logs—it got in the way of their ability to make deliveries on time, make money, or—most importantly—get home, and sometimes to seriously avoid trouble more immediate than DOT. Then typically a driver's logbook would 'catch up' with them, running ahead of what they could legally do, during a forced layover waiting on dispatch and their next load, or after getting home. The other most common way drivers falsified logs (and I never knew anyone who didn't do this) was to shave actual "driving" or "on-duty, not driving" time worked to a bare minimum to still appear reasonable and legal, using a calculator to average miles, and shaving loading and unloading time. A DOT officer might doubt the regularity of averaging 55 mph, anytime you logged "driving," or that you loaded or unloaded in only thirty minutes, but couldn't prove you hadn't, for example—even if you'd been driving 25 mph or less through LA gridlock or a North Dakota blizzard. You were supposed to keep a monthly logbook with no missing pages, but DOT could only legally check or hold you accountable for the last seven working days. The best DOT officers were those who placed safety as the priority and enforced the spirit of the law, and most drivers aspired to professionalism, courtesy, and safety. The worst DOT officers were petty, bitterly cynical, and enforced the letter of the law. The worst drivers were dangerously incompetent, outrageous scofflaws, or knowingly drove dangerous equipment—these were always in the minority, I felt, and one way or another didn't last long. For most drivers and the agents of compliance, we recognized we shared a game in which a wry grin and mutual respect were exchanged, then shared a nod to each other as we danced around the regulations each knowing the other was merely attempting a job which was vital and necessary. The driver was performing a thankless, difficult job, and the DOT was there to ensure and keep everybody safe, up to and including protecting us from ourselves or our dispatchers/employers, not merely the public. On-board computers in trucks and electronic logbooks were becoming more and more the norm for larger outfits and even medium-sized companies.

To some people, fourteen hours of work in a day, five days in a row, might seem like a lot to be working, but consider, when you're not "working" you are stuck somewhere sleeping in a truck's sleeper berth (which to me was still working because I certainly wasn't home with wife and kids, or in my own bed). Not only were you not making money but likely spending "off duty" paying for meals in a town you're unfamiliar with which may or may not be hospitable to your presence— might even be dangerous. Say, if the weather is 40 below, or you're in Philadelphia, NYC, or even Seattle or LA on the wrong side of town and have nowhere to park. Remember, deliveries were always in the worst areas and typically done in the middle of the night. To a person who makes the sacrifice of time away from home and family to work and earn a living by working and sleeping out of their truck, fourteen hours a day might be OK, but the sixty/seventy hour rule is not, especially when you are only paid only when the "wheels are turning" (my typical wage was .25 per mile (early to mid-1990s)—to offer perspective, at 55 mph, rolling, that is $13 per hour—and some folks were paid by the load which most often meant less. The inflexibility of regulations and the bureaucratic clumsiness of one size must fit all did not account for or allow you to plan ahead to outrun storms or bad weather, or make getaways out of Chicago or LA ghettos without sidestepping regulations unless you just happened to have a lot of hours or timing happened to be fortuitous (which was never!). Occasionally the law went counter to the safety of the individual driving the truck, and was always counter-productive to making a living in an already low wage-to-work ratio, but most often it was simply inconvenient. There is a clause in the code stating that if stuck in a snow-storm or unable to find safe-haven to park, you were allowed two extra hours to find it, but no one ever used this clause because it only served to arouse suspicion of DOT officers and internal company compliance auditors who pored over your books all the more carefully whenever it was invoked. Truck drivers become better planners of their routes than any other person who travels for a living. They had to—their livelihood and sometimes their very lives depended on it.

So for the purposes of this poem, I had probably worked something approaching 90 actual hours in a five day period (Sunday afternoon to Friday night) to be unable to 'fudge' my books any further, and find myself in a position I needed to "hand off my rollers" to another driver (Friday morning? I admit this was excessive, but it had been a very unusual week). It should be noted that Jim, as tough as he was, was too old for this job, and probably had smoked for fifty years or more, and not long after I spoke with him, his leg and hip were badly injured by a pallet containing cases of gallon jugs of drinking water that collapsed over on him. Physically, this finished him off, work-wise. The Dollar Tree driving job consisted of hand-unloading a trailer per day that weighed approximately fifty thousand pounds, consisting of three thousand cases on average. Out of the initial crew of eighteen, as far as I know, I was one of two drivers to avoid sustaining serious injuries of one kind or another. The Dollar Tree account paid me something like .38 per mile in 2007 and fifteen dollars per drop (a trailer consisted of usually one to three but sometimes five drops and took seven and a half hours on average to unload by hand. This was hard work. The shortest time I clocked unloading a trailer was four hours, because they had a dock and a full crew that didn't mess around—most lacked this. A typical day was to begin with a loaded trailer at my first drop early in the morning, make my deliveries, then head back to the terminal, drop my empty and pick up my new loaded trailer, then drive to my first drop to be set up for the next day, spend the night, then start over. The territory was Oregon, Washington, Idaho. Occasionally we dipped down into northern California. Right before I left there was talk of expanding into Utah. This was the job. I trained far more drivers who took one look then walked away than those who stuck it out after seeing what the job entailed.

Not the Chicken: The birds might have been turkeys, not chickens. I can't remember and chose not to worry about this.

Sometime After 3 a.m., at the Dollar Tree in Vancouver, WA: This was an Art Bell episode from his late-night talk show, *Coast to Coast AM*. Perhaps like the huge photograph poem, I have mis-remembered important details and names since the details were transcribed from a rough memory without any fact-checking.

Outwitting your Angels: The wolverine trope and details are drawn from an essay by Barry Lopez, *Story at Anaktuvak Pass*, from *The Graywolf Annual Three: Essays, Memoirs & Reflections*, edited by Scott Walker. The wolverine is the fiercest, toughest animal on the planet, closest to man, however wolverines as a species are tougher than most men generally, and while we might be smarter, they are unquestionably fiercer AND tougher. If you go to the trouble of hunting down Lopez's essay, you will note that I've shamelessly lifted narrative details about the wolverine from a story shamelessly lifted and related by Lopez from the hunters from the Brooks Range of Alaska who told it to him. This is how mythology develops from story to legend, then finally becoming myth.

Moonlights: The painter/painting being referenced here is James McNeill Whistler, *Nocturne in Black and Gold—The Falling Rocket* (1875).

Monument: The Lava River Cave near Bend, OR is part of the Newberry National Volcanic Monument.

Mid-January Early Morning Smoke: The setting here is looking from the backyard of The Colonyhouse at Rockaway Beach, OR.

Quiet Night at the Alvord Desert Bath House: I feel it necessary to declare that I have several good friends named Mike, one who actually lives and buckaroos at the Kueny Ranch not far from the bathhouse, but none of my friends are the "Mike" in this poem. Mike Smit, of the Kueny, would never fire a gun into the sky for any reason, even in the wilderness. For one thing, too many people have discovered this amazingly unique place.

Trailer 2542L: This poem is indebted to a short story by Joseph Conrad, *The Brute*, which features a cursed ship, "The Apse Family." Other cursed ship stories are *The Shadow-line*, in which the ship is "haunted" by the previous, deceased captain, and *Youth* in which the voyage is simply cursed (plague, lack of wind, then finally the freight catches fire and consumes the ship). Conrad had a wicked sense of humor.

If all you've ever read is *Heart of Darkness,* you'd never know this. *Typhoon* is laugh out loud funny. Really!

[We the despoilers, the bloodthirsty, corrupt, a few days before Christmas]: The title was adopted ironically in response to a harsh review ("This is bullshit!") from a friend of mine at the online poetry forum *The Critical Poet.*

Acknowledgments

"CB Conversation #2: The Siren Call, Winnemucca, NV," "CB Conversation #3: Flying J Truckstop, North Platte, NE—The I-80 Closure from Pine Bluffs To Rawlins for 36 Hours," "CB Conversation #4: from Walker Lake to Hawthorne, NV, Two Drivers Discuss the Birds and the Bees" previously appeared in *Monkey Bicycle*.

"Outwitting your Angels" awarded third place, Inter-Board Poetry Contest, 2008.

Several poems appeared previously, usually in slightly different versions in the chapbook, *God Truck Nature,* from the chapbook anthology *Burning Gorgeous: Seven 21st Century Poets,* edited by Pamela O'Shaughnessy, Laika Press and Robertson Publishing, 2010.

"Meeting," previously appeared in *Randomly Accessed Poetics*.

"Tiny Apocalypse Behind the Dollar Tree in Lewiston, ID," "Moonlights," "Train, Bird, Man, Behind the Dollar Tree in Milton, WA," and "Huge Photograph of a Logging Crew Hung in Burger King, Near the Dollar Tree in White City, OR" appeared in *An Amazing, Eclectic Anthology*, edited by John F. Garmon and Zend Lakdavala, 2016.

Thanks go out to all the editors of these publications.

I'd like to thank the following for reading and offering invaluable commentary on the manuscript before publication: Zeke Sanchez, Pamela O'Shaughnessy, Bill Jolliff, Mike Geile, Keith Hansen, Richard Engnell, Lynn Otto, and Sally.

Also the writers at the Hornet Court group: Colleen Jeffery, Gina Ochsner, Bernie Meyer, and Geronimo Tagatac.

And all the many poets who posted and commented at *The Critical Poet* over many years.

More recently the Coffee Cottage drive-thru group, and the folks at John Miller's Ars Poetica, and additionally David Memmott and Paul Willis for their review, insights, and helpful commentary on the manuscript. Last minute but very necessary comments made by Mary Giudice and Craig Goodworth.

Joe and Cosette Puckett at Aubade Publishing for inexhaustible patience and flexibility, and professionalism.

Lastly, Z.Z. Wei for his kindness in allowing us to reproduce an image of his painting "Crow" from the *Crow Series* for the cover.

Thank you!

About the Author

David Mehler lives in Newberg, Oregon, moving there with wife and kids in the late 1990s, to take over ownership of Oregon's longest running independent coffeehouse. He is the editor of the literary journal, *Triggerfish Critical Review*. His chapbook, *God Truck Nature* appeared in the chapbook anthology, *Burning Gorgeous: Seven 21st Century Poets*, edited by Pamela O'Shaughnessy (2010). He began serving on the board of the Oregon Poetry Association in the fall of 2019. He is currently at work revising a manuscript of prose poems pertaining to his job as a truck driver for a landfill not far from Portland.

CPSIA information can be obtained
at www.ICGtesting.com
Printed in the USA
BVHW011619151220
595676BV00032B/620